Advance Praise for *Parenting Through Illness*

I strongly recommend this book to parents. Having been the director of school-based health centers for the past twenty years, I know the struggles children have in understanding and talking about their fears when a parent, grandparent or guardian has an illness. *Parenting Through Illness* will help you cope not only with your own fears and apprehensions, but also with how to relate to your child.

—JO ANN DERBONNE, R.N., Director of School Based Health Centers for CHRISTUS Health Central Louisiana.

Children need someone to help guide them through the devastation of their parent's illness and aid them in their journey toward understanding. I fully recommend *Parenting Through Illness* to parents, children, and professionals working and providing medical and mental health services to families facing a serious illness.

—ERIN DUGAN, PH.D., LPC-S, RPT-S, Director LSUHSC New Orleans Child & Family Counseling Clinic

This honest and clear-headed guide is written with both empathy and practical advice, for any parent facing the daunting task of caring for children while ill. Particularly helpful are the summaries that explain how a child's age and development informs that child's reaction to a sick parent—and how a parent can successfully intervene on their child's behalf.

—LEDA SISKIND, LMFT, Mental Health Consultant, La Canada Unified Scho   ⁱ   I   Angeles

Advance Praise for *Parenting Through Illness*

Practical tips, relevant examples, and comforting strategies for families facing crisis. All families are different and all children are different, but Collins and Nathan write about what is *real*, helping all parents focus on what is most important and useful. The *Do's and Don'ts* chapter summaries are like having a cheat sheet.

—JENNI WATTS EVANS, Assistant Director, Parenting Center, Children's Hospital, New Orleans

As a licensed clinician working in a hospital setting, I feel this book will be a great resource to my patients who are parents and who are faced with a life-threatening illness. I especially appreciate how the book highlights the fact that children may not express their emotions in the way adults do or in ways a parent might expect, and offers practical suggestions for parents to create a sense of safety for their children when faced with this crisis.

—JANELLE GOH, LCSW, Supervisor of Social Services, San Joaquin Hospital, Bakersfield, California

Not until I became a cancer surgeon did I realize how difficult it is for children who have a sick parent, and how ill-prepared I was to give advice to either parent or child. This new book provides a guide for dealing with an issue that has been inadequately handled in the past, and should be required reading for medical professionals who deal with serious illnesses.

—ALAN STOLIER, M.D., Center for Restorative Breast Surgery, New Orleans

Advance Praise for *Parenting Through Illness*

I recommend this book both as a physician and as a parent whose spouse experienced a life-threatening illness. The most difficult part of my husband's leukemia was the impact it had on the lives of our children. This excellent guide will help ease your family through the painful journey as you all transition into the "new normal." You can provide for the well being of your children in a way that will positively impact their lives forever.

—JUDITH NANCE, M.D., Family Practice,
Rapides Regional Physician Group

An unexpected illness has the potential to shatter the lives of everyone in the family, but there is hope. Collins and Nathan have masterfully come up with realistic suggestions to aid a grief-stricken family through any kind of illness, including how to help parents process their child's reactions while going through an emotional crisis. Discover tools and research to help you develop a deepened relationship with your children.

—DEREK CLARK, Motivational Speaker, Trainer and Author

PARENTING
THROUGH
ILLNESS
Help for Families When a Parent Is Seriously Ill

Leigh Collins, LCSW and Courtney Nathan, LCSW

HOHM PRESS
Chino Valley, Arizona

Cover Design: Adi Zuccarello, adizuccarello@gmail.com

Interior Design and Layout: Becky Fulker, Kubera Book Design, Prescott, Arizona

Library of Congress Cataloging-in-Publication Data

Names: Collins, Leigh Guillory, author. | Nathan, Susan Courtney | Nathan, Susan Courtney, author.
Title: Parenting through illness : help for families when a parent is seriously ill / Leigh Collins, LCSW and Courtney Nathan, LCSW.
Description: Chino Valley, Arizona : Hohm Press, 2016. | Includes bibliographical references and index.
Identifiers: LCCN 2016016819 (print) | LCCN 2016033370 (ebook) | ISBN 9781942493181 (Print) | ISBN 9781942493259 (ebook) | ISBN 9781942493150 (ebook)
Subjects: LCSH: Children of sick parents. | Parenting. | Sick--Family relationships.
Classification: LCC BF723.P25 C6295 2016 (print) | LCC BF723.P25 (ebook) | DDC 649/.1087--dc23
LC record available at https://lccn.loc.gov/2016016819

Hohm Press
P.O. Box 4410
Chino Valley, AZ 86323
800-381-2700
http://www.hohmpress.com

This book was printed in the U.S.A. on recycled, acid-free paper using soy ink.

We dedicate this book in loving memory of
Dotty Gold Nathan and in honor of our children,
Isabel, Audrey, and Leo.

Acknowledgements

It's hard to believe that we have now been working on this subject together for over ten years. We are as passionate as ever about supporting families coping with a parent's serious illness. We believe strongly in our mission to help parents understand children's developmental and intellectual ability to grasp such a difficult topic. Writing this book has been our honor and privilege, and we hope that it is useful to families everywhere who are struggling to cope with a family illness.

We are grateful to many generous, supportive people without whom we could not have completed this project. First and foremost, we want to thank the brave individuals and families who shared their stories with us. Their openness and generosity of spirit inspired us and gave us valuable insights. Over the years, we have met many wonderful people who have battled serious illnesses with grace and courage. We have used pseudonyms in the book to protect confidentiality, but our participants and their stories are very real and true to us.

We would like to thank the Dora Ferber Foundation and the Louisiana Jewish Endowment Foundation for the grant that initially made this book possible. Thanks, also, to Jewish Family Service of Greater New Orleans, in particular to Lauren Gehman, Eden Heilman and Deena Gerber, former Executive Director of JFS, all of whom read drafts, assisted with focus groups, and encouraged us to pursue this project.

Thanks to Touro Hospital, Robert Gardner and the Heebe Family Fund established in honor of Odom Heebe and the late Mimi Heebe and their children to make life better for children whose parents have cancer. Your support and appreciation of our work and your devotion to sharing it with families in need has been an honor.

We would also like to thank those family, friends and colleagues on whom we called for ideas, direction, and feedback. David Techner, Director of the Kaufman Chapel in Detroit, Michigan, shared his personal and professional experience with us and helped us with the chapter "Coping with Terminal Illness and the Aftermath." Max Nathan, Jr, Courtney's father and our friend, introduced us to experts we would have had a hard time meeting otherwise. Many medical experts helped us. In particular, we would like to thank the doctors at the Louisiana State University Stan Scott Cancer Center and Chris Dvorak, MS, CGC, Genetic Counselor at Tulane University School of Medicine, for sharing their time and expertise.

Many thanks to Rose McCleary and Barbara Reifel from the Social Work Department at California State University, Bakersfield, who read drafts and assisted with the Institutional Review Board (IRB) protocol to conduct research with human subjects.

Finally, none of this would have happened without the support and patience of our husbands, Michael and Richard, and our children, Audrey, Leo, and Isabel. This book was written largely at night and on weekends, and our devotion to it sometimes meant time and attention taken away from our families. We are lucky that all of you understand our love for this book and the importance our work holds for us. We are grateful every day for all of you.

Contents

Getting the Diagnosis

Sally and Ed's Story

Sally was thirty-five when she was diagnosed with breast cancer. Her doctor found a lump during a routine check-up, but he reassured her that it probably wasn't anything serious. Sally felt only slightly concerned. She thought to herself that she was too young and healthy for it to be anything dangerous. Besides that, she was happily married with two young children who needed her. Surely she couldn't have cancer.

The biopsy revealed that the lump was malignant. When she heard the news, she felt overwhelming dread. "My first thought was that I was going to throw up," she says. "I thought, 'Oh my God. This can't be real. This can't be happening. What am I going to do? What are my children going to do?' Then I started to realize that I might die."

Sally sat in her doctor's office, too shocked to drive herself home or even to cry. The doctor called her husband, Ed, and Sally waited, wondering what would happen next. Would she need surgery? Chemotherapy and radiation treatments? What would happen to her three-year-old daughter and her five-year-old son? What if she died?

Sally spent a good hour in the doctor's office, trying to absorb the news. When Ed arrived, he just held her hand and cried quietly. He asked the doctor some questions about treatment, but mostly he was preoccupied with his own fears, wondering, "What is going to happen to my beautiful wife? To our family and the kids? Can I handle this? What am I going to do?"

Five years later, Sally's cancer has been in remission for two years. She and her husband report that they did find ways to handle the challenges brought on by her illness, but it was not easy. Sally says, "We fought more than ever because we were both so stressed out. I resented Ed because I thought he should be doing more to take care of me when I was feeling so bad. Sometimes I resented the kids because they still had needs, and they expected their mommy to take care of them. Part of my resentment was really just guilt that I couldn't do everything they wanted me to do. It took some time to recover, not only from the illness itself, but also from the emotional repercussions."

For Ed, the biggest challenge was taking over many of Sally's parenting duties when she was too sick to take care of them herself. He says, "I think I handled the daily tasks pretty well, but the main thing I had trouble with was talking to the children about what was going on with their mom. One time Sally was hospitalized, and I knew the kids were scared and worried, but I felt paralyzed to help them. Sally always talked to them about how they were feeling, but I honestly didn't know how to discuss something so serious with such young kids. I wanted to, but it didn't seem possible. Sally and I talked about it and realized that what we both wanted most was to keep our kids safe and happy. We each did the best we could under the circumstances even though, at times, we both felt like we were failing."

Introduction

A t its heart, this book is about parenting. Although by nature a very personal and private matter, the effect of a parent's serious illness on the family is far-reaching. Most children, particularly young ones, expect their parents to be able to solve any problem and to take care of them no matter what. Naturally, as a parent you want to meet the challenge, but a serious illness will probably entail some big changes in how you take care of your children. Just when you feel most vulnerable and grief-stricken, your children need you to be strongest for them. Just as your own fears of mortality threaten to overwhelm you, your children need you to assure them that you will survive. Before you can meet your children's needs, you must first garner all your strength and resources.

Think of it this way: each time you board an airplane, you're informed that, in the event of an emergency, you should provide yourself with oxygen before attempting to help others. When faced with a serious illness, you need to care for yourself first in order to be able to care for your children. In this book we explore why that can be extremely difficult, and we suggest ways to do it.

If you're like most parents, one of your greatest fears is that something bad will happen to your children. Like Sally and Ed in the story preceding this chapter, your instinct is to protect your children at all costs. Sometimes that's not possible. If you're reading this book, chances are something is now happening to you, and you have to cope with that reality.

When you learned that you had a serious illness, your initial thoughts were probably about what the illness would mean for you. Most people wonder how, and if, they can fight the illness, how it will affect their bodies and minds, and whether or not they might die. Thoughts about how the illness will affect the family often come later; that's normal and natural.

Most parents know that their own death would be a huge crisis in their children's lives. They also know that a serious illness, even if not potentially fatal, would change the lives of everyone in the family, at least temporarily.

Having lived through my own mother's struggle with breast cancer, I know firsthand how devastating such an illness can be on a family. I know how easy it is for children to misinterpret symptoms and behavior. I know how easy it is for children to ignore or run away from a parent's illness. I know the kinds of questions that go unasked and unanswered, and that the failure to talk about these questions may have lifelong consequences. I also know that even excellent parents can struggle to cope and respond to their children. While there is no protecting any of us from the pain and uncertainty that a life-threatening illness brings to a family, this guide may help families develop some tools for coping with this difficult challenge.

One legacy of my experience with my mother's illness is an unceasing concern about my own health, especially now that I am a mother myself. One of my greatest fears is that I will leave my children motherless, as my mother left me. On the day I learned I was pregnant, I began writing letters to my daughter so that she should have a sense of who I am and the way I think and feel in case I'm not here to tell her and show her myself. Anne Roiphe has explored this conflict in Fruitful *(Penguin, 1996, 77), saying of motherhood,*

There is always the fear of death. When my children were young it came over me all the time. I could not bear to think of them grieving for me. I could not bear to think of them missing me. I was afraid to fly. From liftoff to touchdown I thought of them needing and not having a mother and I would imagine their loss in specific detail. In those days, I would worry about car accidents, mutating cells, sudden strokes, slowly debilitating nerve diseases, all because I could not tolerate the idea of my children hurt the way my death would hurt them.

— Courtney Nathan

In this book we focus on living through an illness. Our hope, of course, is that you will enjoy a full recovery and a long and healthy life. We also hope that your children will weather the crisis of your illness and emerge happy and strong. But experience has taught us that no matter how well children are prepared and how successful they are at coping, a parent's illness is always life-altering.

As therapists and mothers, we look at parenting from both a professional and a personal perspective. We have watched families navigate their way through disease, treatment, and recovery. We have seen loving, involved families pretend that an illness doesn't exist or doesn't matter. We've seen intelligent, sensitive, and well-intentioned parents go numb in the face of personal, shocking, and devastating crises. We've watched parents and children struggle to incorporate into their minds and lives scary information that is hard to understand. We've heard highly successful parents and even doctors claim (mistakenly) that children don't need to know about a parent's illness because it's a "grownup thing" and will only cause them undue stress. We know that, in most instances, they are wrong.

The difference between the ways children and adults express themselves during a crisis is one reason we fail to pick up on the sadness, anger, or other difficult emotions they have in coping with the illness of a loved one. Many people worry that their own reactions or their children's, might be bizarre, weird, or just plain wrong. The reality is that many reactions—odd as they may appear during normal times—are perfectly appropriate during trying times. Sometimes the questions children come up with are shocking, upsetting, or difficult to answer.

We explore how children of different ages express and deal with these strong emotions. What children understand and how they react to their parent's illness depends largely on their maturity. That's why we address the differences of the reactions of children of varying ages, from young children to preteens and teenagers. There is a wide range of what may be considered "normal" depending on their age. We have tried to demonstrate this range by providing anecdotal information as well as examples of questions that a child from each age group might ask, along with sample responses.

While preparing this book, we searched for resources already available to parents and hospitals. Every computer or library search yielded many books for parents whose children were seriously ill, but very little for parents who were ill themselves and needed help on how to care for their children during this crisis. This lack of information highlights an important point: children are disadvantaged as grievers. We have tried to remedy this lack by providing an accessible book with practical tips for parents facing what may be the greatest emotional crisis of their lives.

Throughout the book, we have based our information on years of extensive research, including many individual interviews and focus groups with both children and adults. We have also drawn from our professional experience as clinical social workers specializing in work with children and families. We hope that our experience has been helpful in providing this guide through the difficult journey that parents must navigate when raising their children while coping with a serious illness.

The Stages of Grief

In her classic book *On Death and Dying* (1969), Elisabeth Kübler-Ross outlined the emotions most people go through when they experience any serious loss, including a death. We outline these stages here because most people experience these feelings, to one degree or another, when they are seriously ill or when someone they love is seriously ill. While these stages are listed in the order that Kübler-Ross felt that they presented themselves, most people do not experience them in this exact sequence. You may, for example, continue to revisit emotions you thought you had already worked through.

Stage 1: Denial and Isolation

This is a temporary state of shock in which you may feel numbness and disbelief. Denial is common to almost all grieving individuals for a period, especially initially. It can be useful because it can serve as a buffer to help you handle shocking news without being completely overwhelmed by the intensity of your emotions.

Stage 2: Anger

When you can no longer deny the reality of your loss, it is normal to feel anger, rage, envy, and resentment. This is the stage when you ask, "Why me?" You may become angry with yourself, your family, friends, physicians, even God.

Stage 3: Bargaining

Bargaining often involves trying to make some sort of agreement with God or any higher power to somehow postpone, alter, or minimize the loss. You may find yourself wondering whether you can put off or end your illness if you are "good" or if you make certain promises. For example, a wife may suggest that if her husband can be cured of his illness, she will never get angry with him again. Most bargains are made with a higher power and are kept secret.

Stage 4: Depression

Denial, anger, and bargaining may be replaced by depression when you begin to realize the magnitude of your loss, including the effects on your life, whether these effects be physical, emotional, financial, social, or occupational. Depression can be either anticipatory or reactive. Anticipatory depression occurs when you feel sadness about the losses that may come, while reactive depression occurs as a direct response to an actual loss.

Stage 5: Acceptance

If you are able to work through your feelings of loss, you will eventually come to a place where you no longer feel depressed or angry, even though you have a full awareness of the losses you have suffered. This stage is characterized by a decrease in the intensity of negative emotions and a feeling of acceptance, if not peace.

1. Coming Face to Face with Your Illness

Coming to terms with a serious diagnosis usually involves going through the grief process described above in "The Stages of Grief." You may find that you experience some or all of the emotions noted here—like anger or sadness. You may experience other feelings as well—fear, for example—because there are any number of potential reactions to learning you have a serious medical condition. For some people, the initial disbelief remains while they drift through treatments and surgeries. Like being on auto-pilot, they simply get through the work of treatment before they deal with the emotional reality. As one mother put it, "I really didn't even think about the fact that I had cancer until I was finished with all of the treatments. I was just so focused on fighting it."

Denial is not necessarily a bad thing. It can protect you from the intensity of your emotions. You want to make sure, though, that denial does not affect your ability to take care of yourself and your children. Angela, a young mother with breast cancer, said,

As soon as I was diagnosed, I felt like I was free falling. Right before I ate dust, you know, like in the cartoons, I thought to myself, "I need to come up with a game plan." The next week I was flying from New Orleans to California to leave my kids with my mom. Once I knew that my kids were safe, I entered a stage of denial where I pretended that nothing was wrong. If I hadn't pretended to myself that everything was okay, I wouldn't have been able to get out of bed.

You may also feel vulnerable as you try to deal with what appears to be a total lack of control over your life. It's normal to feel a sense of dread about the future and confusion about things that suddenly seem to be out of your control, including your physical wellbeing, your mortality, and your children's welfare. In response to feelings of uncertainty, some parents become fiercely determined and go directly into fighter mode, thinking, "I won't leave my kids!" For others, hearing their diagnosis is like a bomb going off, splintering their world into sharp, dangerous pieces. Both are normal reactions to a stressful situation. As time goes on, you should realize that much more is in your control than seems true at first. For example, you may think that mundane activities are irrelevant, but you will begin to learn that many of the decisions you make that apparently have nothing to do with your illness, such as picking out your children's clothes, making a grocery list, or ordering a birthday gift, will have a direct effect on your health. With this recognition comes the awareness that it's time to get down to the important business of managing your illness and minimizing its negative effects on the lives of your children. Beth, a mother of three with cancer, noted,

I was aware enough to see that how I handled the whole thing would affect how everyone around me would handle it. I was in control here. My doing well and being comfortable with the whole situation would make my parents and kids more comfortable, and that would then circle back around to me and make it easier on me.

Whatever your reaction is to your diagnosis, it is important to work out some of your anger, resentment, sadness, or fear outside of the presence of your children. This is true no matter how old your children are, but it is especially true for young children who are more likely to be frightened when witnessing strong emotions. Getting your diagnosis may feel like being handed a death sentence, but your life is not over. Although you are bound to feel sad and frightened, remember that there is always hope: that is the main message you will want to impart to your children.

If you need to break down and express your fears, go ahead and do it; that's a healthy part of coping. Talk to any adult you feel comfortable with—your partner, friend, therapist, support group—but avoid burdening your children with your strong negative feelings. It is okay to tell your children that you are scared and sad or to cry with them, but they need to see you fight, too. One teenager whose mother is a cancer survivor said, "When my mom was diagnosed with breast cancer, I will never forget her telling me she was scared. It helped me to understand how serious the diagnosis was. Otherwise, I think I would have been confused about the severity of the illness."

If you find that you are experiencing debilitating depression, seek professional help and consider being evaluated for antidepressant medication to get you through the crisis. Some symptoms of depression include the inability to get out of bed, difficulty falling or staying asleep, an excessive need for sleep, uncontrollable crying, significant changes in appetite, and increased irritability. Remember to talk with your physician to ensure that your symptoms are not a result of your illness or any medication you are taking. In Chapter 7, we offer suggestions for selecting a therapist for your child. Much of that information may also apply to finding your own therapist. The important thing to remember is that *you must never rely on your child, no matter what his or her age or maturity level, as a substitute therapist.*

Children primarily need to feel safe. For this to happen, they need to be able to lean on you without fearing they will hurt or upset you. Let them know that they can talk to you about their feelings, even if it makes you both cry. What you are facing as a family is traumatic, and everyone copes with trauma differently.

Most children, upon learning that their parent is facing a serious illness, worry that their parent may not survive. Some children may ask you directly if you are going to die from this illness. Young children may not have the language skills to ask, or they may not have enough experience to know that death is a possibility. Even if this thought has not occurred to your child, it is not a bad idea to address it directly. For a young child, you might want to say something like, "Sometimes kids worry when a parent is sick that their parent might die. I don't think that will happen to me because I plan to take very good care of myself and do what the doctor tells me to do."

You might want to ask your preteens or teens directly if they are worried that you might die. Adolescents may avoid asking this question because of an unwillingness to expose their own vulnerability. If your illness is not terminal, you can reassure them by giving some medical statistics about your illness and outlining details about your treatment. If your illness could be terminal, do not tell your children otherwise. As much as you want to reassure them, a false answer now could cause them confusion, anger, or distrust later on. You can reassure them, though, by giving them information about how you plan to take care of yourself and general information about your treatment.

Coming to Terms with Your Illness

A serious illness represents a great upheaval to both your body and your psyche. It is crucial that you have a support system. This may include family, friends, colleagues, support groups, school communities, mental health professionals, clergy, or anyone else who can provide comfort and security for you during this time. This support system will help in two major areas: coping with the emotions that follow a diagnosis and organizing your family's daily life with your health and medical needs in mind.

Let's start with the emotions. Learning that you have a life-threatening illness usually involves the acknowledgement of multiple losses—not only the loss of physical health, but also the loss of stability, security, normalcy, sense of future, financial security, and more. Again, the five stages of grief outlined previously can provide a useful framework to help you identify the losses you are experiencing and the related emotions.

Take some time after hearing the diagnosis to gather your thoughts and put your situation in perspective, keeping in mind that your perspective could change frequently throughout your illness. It's okay to ask for help, even if you're not used to either asking for it or accepting it. For example, one mother had an illness that confined her to the house. When her friends inquired what they could do for her, she asked if they would drive her children to school and sports practice, the one thing she was truly unable to do. Her relief at being able to stay home and take care of herself, knowing that her children's needs were being met, was incalculable.

Even if it goes against your grain, accepting help with household and childcare responsibilities may be necessary, particularly when you are weak or taking medication. Relying on others can be difficult, and it is normal to feel angry or resentful as you watch others, even your spouse or partner, take over your duties and experience the satisfaction that comes from meeting these responsibilities. These feelings usually pass with time, though. It may help to remind yourself that you will be able to resume your responsibilities once you are feeling better.

From time to time you may find that you are angry about a lot of things that, on the surface, seem inconsequential. Anger is a normal and acceptable emotion, and you should expect to feel it at times when faced with a medical crisis. You may also lash out in anger when you are actually feeling a different emotion, such as sadness, fear, or panic that may be too painful to experience head on. Sometimes it helps just to remind yourself that you are really angry about your illness, not about something a family member did. One woman told us, "The best advice I ever got about how to deal with my illness was 'Don't take it out on the ones you love.' After everything we've been through, I'm sure my family is still together, in large part, because I reminded myself of that every day." If you sense that your anger is becoming uncontrollable or seriously affecting the way you treat your family, you might want to consult a counselor to help you sort through your feelings.

Now for practical matters. If your illness or treatment will prevent you from being able to care for your children for a time, you need to arrange for their basic needs to be met. Call upon the people who care about you to pick up the routines at home until you establish new routines that work for you. Consider selecting one person to be responsible for duties that directly affect your children, to provide some consistency for your family. Even if this person delegates responsibilities to others, he or she will be the "go-to" in times of need. Remember, many people will offer to help, but few will truly know what you need from them. Don't rely on them "taking the hint." Now is the time to state clearly what you need and want them to do, whether it is driving carpool, cooking meals, cleaning house, or taking you to the doctor. Be specific: people can't know what you need unless you tell them.

You can ask your children to help you do some of the things you are temporarily unable to do for them, but monitor your expectations. Your five-year-old is probably perfectly capable of pouring a bowl of cereal for breakfast, and your teen can drive your younger children to baseball practice. A pre-teen or teen can also begin cooking some meals for the family. School-age children can start loading the dishwasher every night and making their own beds every morning. Taking on these duties can give them some sense of empowerment and control during a time when they feel out of control. But the overall management of the household, childcare decisions, and delegation of duties should *always* be handled by adults.

Children of all ages can help, and appreciate knowing that they are being helpful. If, however, they are asked to act like little adults, other areas of their lives will suffer. As one woman recalls of her mother's illness,

> *Too much was expected of me at seventeen. My father owned a restaurant, and, when my mom got sick, it was his busiest season, and he didn't have enough help. He asked me to take over the place, so he could take care of my mom, and I felt obligated because, in addition to mom being sick, my dad was really falling apart. Early on, I just lost it at the cash register, and I felt so embarrassed and ashamed afterwards. I continued to run the place for the entire summer in order to help my dad and, like most teens, I never shared any of what I was going through with my parents. I remember*

*feeling really mad at my dad and at our extended family
and friends of the family who didn't see that I was doing too
much, and I just couldn't handle it.*

Every now and then check in with your children and
ask them if any of the chores they have been given are too
burdensome. Remember, your children may not tell you that
they are overwhelmed with their responsibilities, so it's also
up to you to pay attention and ask yourself if the increased
household duties are interfering with schoolwork or preventing
your children from playing or spending time with friends.

Taking Care of Yourself

Many parents have a strong need to stay positive. But some
of the obvious outlets, like therapy, support groups, and self-
help books, just don't work for everyone. Some people we've
talked to say that even *considering* these options makes them
feel depressed and overwhelmed. One mother, who tried
Internet support chat rooms, said that hearing about others'
experiences made her more hopeless and scared. Another said,
"The hospital gave me two social workers. I'm sure that's good
for other people, but I didn't want to talk to strangers. I was
very standoffish. Then, once I started chemo, I was assigned
yet another social worker. I felt like they were assigned to me
because the hospital thought I was dying. I wanted to handle
it on my own." If you try something and it is not helpful, try
something else. Trust your instincts. What works for one person
may not work for you. Seek an outlet that seems right for you.

Many parents are determined not to let their illness rule
their lives. One father with multiple sclerosis explained, "I didn't
want my illness to be the focus of my children's lives. I wanted

to hear them talk about school and their friends." Initially, your illness probably will and should be the primary focus of your attention. However, if you make an effort to concentrate on other experiences and areas of your life, you may experience more energy and balance. So will your children.

To the best of your ability, continue to participate in the interests and activities you were involved in before you got sick. Maintaining a hobby or taking up a new one can provide a positive distraction. Exercise, yoga, Pilates, or a new sport can be great for you, both physically and psychically. Meditation, walking, and reading can all be relaxing and effective ways for you to take care of yourself. Even if you don't think you can afford it, consider indulging in a spa service like a massage or a manicure now and then, and remind yourself that you deserve time to refuel in whatever ways you find enjoyable.

In addition to the stress of coping with your illness, you will also be dealing with the normal stress of parenting. As if parenting under normal conditions weren't taxing enough, suddenly you have to add doctor visits, tests, treatments, and physical challenges. *Remember, you are experiencing a major trauma, and your life will not just go on as usual.* For both parents, and children, this can be a difficult fact to accept. Mothers in particular often expect to be able to do everything and be everything to everyone all the time. We cannot emphasize this point enough: you do not need to be ashamed to ask for the help you need.

Some parents may fear that they are "bad parents" because they are sick. This just isn't true. You didn't choose to get sick, and you will fight the disease as best you can. You may believe that giving up some of your duties at home means neglecting your family. One mother said, "Not being able to take my kids to school in the morning because I couldn't get out of bed was so disheartening." But the reality is that your life has changed on every level, and you are doing everything you can to get your strength back so that you can resume your normal routine and responsibilities.

You are bound to feel a sense of urgency, so try to manage your time wisely. Don't allow yourself to be tied to social responsibilities. Avoid spending more time than you want to on the phone or with visitors. Don't overextend yourself in an effort not to seem rude or because you're grateful that people care about you. It is crucial that you make taking care of yourself and your family a priority, and recognize that doing so is neither rude nor selfish. If talking on the phone encourages you, do it. If it causes you stress, come up with other ways to keep friends and family informed. One parent whose wife was ill saved time by sending group emails every few days, updating friends and family on his wife's progress with stem-cell replacement. Group emails, texts, and social media and care sites are increasingly popular ways for families to communicate with large groups about a loved one's illness. We will explore this option more thoroughly in Chapter 6.

Other people may not always recognize the internal havoc your illness is wreaking on your body because you appear the same on the outside. It can be difficult when they don't understand how sick you are. It can also be confusing for your children. A mother with lupus described her frustration with her friends and her children who seemed irritated when she could not participate in various activities because she looked okay to them. Your symptoms may fluctuate, and you may be able to do some things one day but not the next. Be patient with your children and explain that, while you may look healthy, you are indeed sick and need rest. Even though your illness isn't always visible, it's really there, and you need to take care of yourself.

Illness and Spirituality

Times of crisis can evoke strong spiritual considerations. Even if you were not religious before, you may now find yourself grappling with existential questions about life, death, and God. Your children may also have spiritual or religious concerns, doubts, and questions. They may wonder why and how your illness happened, and they may question God's will or existence. They may also have strong personal reactions to your own spiritual questions. Some people might doubt another's authenticity or honesty when he or she turns to religion during a time of crisis. But, as many people find comfort in faith, just because you or your children may not have been spiritual before does not mean you cannot turn to religion now. On the other hand, it is also natural to question one's own faith, or that of others, when in crisis. Feelings of betrayal in this spiritual domain are akin to those experienced during the stages of grief about your condition in general, and you can be confident that it is your right to work through a spiritual "dark night of the soul" just as you are working through your illness.

Your children are used to looking to you for answers, or at least they expect you to be able to find answers or point them in the right direction even if you don't have them yourself. Your own lack of religious certainty and your inability to soothe your children's spiritual concerns may frustrate you. It's okay to admit that there are things you don't understand or can't explain and to acknowledge that your uncertainty might be frustrating to them. If you find a spiritual leader comforting, seek his or her guidance. Talk over your concerns with your mate or a close friend. Simply wondering out loud about the meaning of life can sometimes bring comfort. Exploring some new spiritual practice such as meditation might be helpful too. Do what gives you more peace, more confidence, but don't expect to find all the answers all at once.

Getting Financial Assistance

A medical crisis can precipitate a financial crisis as well. One woman whose treatments created serious financial hardships for her family told us,

> *My husband tells me it was worth every penny to still have me here. I'm grateful for his attitude, but it's overwhelming because I can't see how we will ever pay it all off. In the heat of the moment, we were worried about getting better, not about the financial hit. I would not have done it differently, though. No regrets. I just wish there were more ways to help people financially.*

Even if you are not the sole source of income for your family, you may worry about how high medical costs and potential loss of income will affect your ability to make ends meet. Treatment costs can be devastatingly high. Unfortunately, most communities offer only limited resources to families facing financial emergencies. As one woman noted,

> *I contacted the American Cancer Society and other organizations to see if there was any way I could get financial assistance to purchase prosthetic breasts. Every group I contacted said I made too much money to qualify for aid. That was frustrating, because over the years we*

have donated a lot of money, but when we needed help we couldn't get it.

If you have trouble paying your bills during your illness, here are some options to consider:

- Talk with your employer about sick leave and other options, including flex-time, telecommuting, and working at home. Also find out if your employer's insurance includes a disability policy.

- Hospital social workers should be able to advise you. At the very least, they should be able to help you apply for Medicaid if you are eligible. Medicaid is the largest program in the United States that provides medical and health-related services to low-income individuals and families. Benefits and requirements of this program, which is a joint venture of federal and state governments, vary from state to state. (See the list of "Resources" in Appendix B for contact information and websites.)

- The Affordable Care Act (ACA) is meant to provide health care that is high quality, affordable, and accessible to everyone. If you do not have adequate health insurance coverage, this may be an option for you. If you are uninsured, there may be tax penalties for not applying for coverage. You can apply for coverage in various ways; visit *www.healthcare.gov* for more information.

- Hospitals may refer you to the public hospital system if you have financial constrictions.

- Some hospitals have separate, private funds available to help families in need, but these generally offer only small amounts. Be sure to inquire about your options.

- The cost of medicine is often a burden. Your doctor may give you free drug samples or refer you to a pharmaceutical program that sells medications at lower prices.

- Various community agencies offer a wide range of help, based on meeting certain guidelines. Many religious institutions, the YMCA/YWCA, the Council on Aging, United Way agencies, and other nonprofit groups offer various types of assistance including money for utilities, rent, medicine, medical costs, transportation, and food. They may also be able to provide low-cost assistance in other areas such as home health care and homemaker services.

- Religious institutions often have discretionary funds to help families in need.

- Ask your hospital social worker about applying for Social Security Disability (SSD) or Supplemental Security Income (SSI). SSD benefits are available to individuals who have worked for several years, while SSI benefits are paid to those who are poor or disabled even if they have not worked recently. If you want to apply for SSD or SSI, you may want to consult with an attorney who specializes in this area. The application process for disability can be painstakingly difficult, and people often get rejected and must reapply. In fact, according to the Social Security Disability Legal Help website, approximately 70 percent of initial claims are rejected, and the claims process can take up to one and a half years to complete. Experienced lawyers can often speed this process along.

- One of the most important things to remember is that, *to receive financial help from the hospital, you must ask for assistance from hospital personnel.* Once you inform them, they will either help you themselves or refer you to appropriate professionals who can guide you through the process.

- If your treatment requires you to travel, reach out to the hospital social worker with questions about affordable housing options and travel assistance.

Facing Legal Issues and Guardianship

Most people facing a serious illness recover with treatment. Still, it's important to be prepared for any outcome. We suggest that you make a will, if you have not already done so, and consider who would be the best guardians for your children in your absence. Though these issues are hard to think about, you will feel more in control of your situation if you take steps to ensure that your children will be cared for in the event that you and your partner can no longer do so. If you are a single parent with a serious illness, you have an even more pressing need to address these issues and may need to move quickly to create a plan for taking care of your children. It is a real challenge to think about these issues, to discuss them with your children, and to make plans for something everyone desperately hopes will not happen. The only thing more difficult is living with the fear of what might happen if you don't make these plans or discuss them.

Some questions to consider concerning wills and guardianship are:

- Do you have a will?

- Do you have a living will?

- Do you want your will to include a directive to inform your children about any genetic testing you have had or any hereditary factors that may affect their health?

- Do you have custody issues that need to be resolved?

- Have you appointed a legal guardian for your child?

- Have you put your custody and guardianship decisions in writing and spoken with all concerned parties?

Although a will consists simply of a written, dated, witnessed, and signed statement of your wishes, you might want to consider meeting with an attorney to help you draft one. You can make a living will with an attorney, or your hospital can help you make one. A living will allows you to specify whether you want hospital personnel to use life support as part of your care, and allows you to appoint someone to make medical decisions about your care in the event that you cannot do so yourself. Some reasons to make a will include:

- To state explicitly your wishes for your child regarding guardianship

- To protect your child from anyone who might interfere with your wishes

- To avoid family battles and misunderstandings

- To delineate clearly to whom you wish to make financial and personal bequests

People sometimes experience either direct or indirect pressure from their families to select someone in particular as guardian, even if they know that person might not be the best one for the job. A seriously ill woman was asked by her sister: "If you die, the children will live with me, right?" This parent actually wanted her children to live with their grandparents but felt pressured to abide by her sister's wishes. Remember, you have the right to choose the person you believe will best care for your children.

Choosing Your Children's Guardian

- *Consider Age:* What is the age of the person you are considering? Is the person old enough to make mature decisions for your children? Is this person young enough to have the energy to care for active children?

- *Consider Asking Your Children's Opinions:* If your children are preteens or older, you may want to discuss with them their thoughts about whom they would want to be their guardian and why. Keep in mind that your children may have a negative reaction to anyone they perceive as taking the place of a parent. You may not want to discuss this with very young children because it might put too much pressure on them or frighten them unnecessarily.

Your children may have specific concerns about what will happen to them if you die. If they are old enough to grasp what you are telling them (even if they can't completely comprehend this complex issue), be honest about the arrangements you have made. Reassure them that, if something should happen to you, their other parent will continue to take care of them. If you choose a different guardian, explain why. If the chosen guardian is not the other parent, avoid making negative statements to explain your choice.

Dos and Don'ts for Coming Face to Face with Your Illness

- *Do* find ways to take some control over your life. Establishing a daily ritual, such as journal writing, meditating, or walking, is helpful.

- *Do* get an organizer, old-fashioned notebook, or smartphone app to track your appointments and treatments.

- *Do* schedule quiet time and fun family activities.

- *Do* talk about your feelings with other adults.

- *Don't* express hopelessness around your children, even if you are feeling that way.

- *Do* tell your children about your sadness and listen to their feelings, but also let them know you are strong enough for them to lean on.

- *Do* allow yourself to grieve for the many changes in your life, including your previous sense of stability.

- *Do* remind yourself that your old life is not over forever; in most cases, you'll resume the things you love to do as soon as you're feeling better.

- *Do* look for constructive ways to cope with intense feelings.

- *Do* provide a consistent routine for your children.

- *Do* choose one adult to handle childcare responsibilities while you're out of commission.

- *Don't* be afraid to ask your child to begin handling some age-appropriate duties.

- *Do* be careful that any duties your child assumes don't detract from schoolwork or social time, and be sure that the management of the household, childcare decisions, and the delegation of duties are always handled by adults.

- *Don't* overextend yourself by returning phone calls or receiving visitors when you don't feel up to it.

- *Don't* expect to do what you used to do in the same amount of time or with the same energy.

- *Don't* try to do more than you can do because others expect it of you.

- *Do* talk about existential or spiritual questions with a spiritual advisor.

- *Don't* beat yourself up if you experience doubts or lose your faith in God temporarily.

- *Don't* feel guilty if you are not a spiritual person.

- *Do* clarify your options with your employer about sick leave and schedule changes.

- *Do* investigate all financial assistance options including SSI, SSD, Medicaid, ACA, public hospitals, pharmaceutical company programs, and agency programs.

- *Do* make a written document of who you want to care for your child if you cannot do so, and outline your child's emergency information and daily routine.

- *Do* talk with an attorney to write a will if you don't already have one.

- *Don't* assume someone else will handle legal issues for you or that legal issues won't matter.

- *Do* consider carefully who would be the best guardian for your children, taking into account your children's opinions.

2. Going It Alone: Special Concerns for the Single Parent

If you are a single parent, you will face all of the challenges mentioned in the previous chapter and more. You may need to call upon friends, family, or community support to help you manage your family life through this crisis and ensure that your children's needs are met. Jill pointed out how difficult that can be as a single mother:

> It's hard enough to be a single parent when you're healthy, but when I was going through my treatments, I wasn't able to do even the simplest things, like going to the grocery store or cooking dinner. Without someone else there to help, I was totally overwhelmed and felt like a terrible parent. I called on my siblings to help me with a lot because, while you may be able to postpone playing Candyland with your kids, things like dinner have to get done.

This is a critical time to be clear with people about your needs. If someone makes a general offer to help, let them know in no uncertain terms what they can do—be specific. You may want to designate one "point person" so that friends and family have someone to contact when they want to offer help or get information. Your point person will provide more consistency and stability for your children as well.

On an emotional level, you're probably feeling pretty overwhelmed. In addition to the grief and fear most people experience after a diagnosis, a serious illness can cause old pains to resurface for a single parent. If you are widowed or divorced, your grief over previous losses or conflicts can return suddenly and unexpectedly. Claire, a cancer survivor and mother of two, told us, "All I could think about during my hospitalization was that, if my jerk of an ex-husband hadn't left me, I wouldn't have to completely depend on my friends to take care of my kids until I got home."

Your children may also have emotional reactions toward their other parent that are triggered by your illness. These can include feelings of anger or, conversely, idealization. If your child fears you may die, she may begin clinging to her other parent out of desperation, regardless of what their relationship was like before you became ill. Even children who have adjusted well to a divorce or death may develop renewed feelings of fear of abandonment, sadness, anxiety about the future, and anger. Talk with your child about her feelings about your illness and about her other parent. Ask whether her feelings about her other parent have changed as a result of your illness. Try to put your own feelings aside and just listen to her. For instance, if you are still angry at an ex, and your child seems to be idealizing him all of a sudden, remind yourself that this is a normal reaction to the fear and insecurity she is feeling. Assure your child that you love her, that you accept whatever feelings she's experiencing, and that you are doing everything possible to keep her safe. She will probably be worried about what changes will take place in her life because of your illness, and these feelings can be particularly intense if there were major changes in the past as a result of divorce or death.

There are also some practical considerations you'll want to discuss with your child. It's possible that, because you're single, your child might need to take more responsibility for dealing with your medical emergencies. Naturally, an infant or toddler can't be relied upon to call an ambulance or even to get a neighbor if there's an emergency, so, as much as possible, have backup plans in place. If it's even remotely possible that your child might be stranded, with you too sick to get help, ask a friend or relative to call or drop by to check on you regularly. You may also want to look into getting an emergency response system in your home. Your hospital or physician should be able to help you arrange to have a system installed that would give you some reassurance that if something happened while you were alone with your young child, someone would be alerted immediately.

If your child is old enough to understand the basic idea of how to cope in an emergency, make sure you sit down with her and talk about what she should do if one happens. Keep a list of emergency phone numbers by the telephone. This list might include your own address and phone number, your doctor's and family members' names and phone numbers, as well as any other emergency numbers. Make the list big and bold so that it's easy to read. Better yet, encode the numbers in a one-touch dialing system, and teach your child how to use it. You can program your doctor's number and an emergency contact into your smartphone as well. Make sure your child has memorized your address and directions to your house, and knows whom to call in the event of an emergency. Check the address numbers on the outside of your house or apartment building to be sure that they are clearly visible from the street and that they are easy to see at night. If your child is young, use dolls or stuffed animals to practice what to do if you or anyone else passes out or falls and is hurt. Review the emergency plan with all of your children from time to time.

Once you have made your plans concerning your physical and family needs, talk to your child about them so that she'll know what to expect regarding your treatment. Let her know which adults may be playing a more active part in your daily routines during your illness. Ask if she has any questions, and try to answer them as honestly as you can. Your child will need assurance that she will be safe and protected. This discussion may be upsetting for your child, so make sure to include lots of physical affection and attention to her feelings.

When You Are Divorced

If you are a single parent because of divorce, you may have a wide range of conflicting feelings. Your grief over your divorce may resurface and get confused with your grief over your illness.

If you have a good working relationship with your ex, you may feel comfortable asking him or her to play a larger role in the daily life of your family during your illness. Often, when one parent is ill, the other parent needs to participate more in such things as carpool, school events, holidays, and family activities. They may have to keep the children more frequently and for longer periods. Sometimes single parents have trouble asking for this kind of help, either because they feel it won't be forthcoming or because of resentment and unresolved feelings. As one divorced mother put it,

> *I felt like I had no choice but to call on my ex-husband to help with carpooling the kids and staying with them when I had to go to the doctor, but it was really hard because I have such angry feelings left over toward him from our divorce. I had to really suck it up and do what I thought was best for the children.*

24

It may help to schedule a few sessions with a mediator or counselor to discuss in a neutral setting what you need from your ex-spouse. Some other ideas may include writing a letter to your ex-spouse explaining your situation, or enlisting the help of a relative or friend who may be able to guide you and support you in approaching your ex. Think seriously about whether it's time to put aside your differences with your ex to make things easier for yourself and your children.

In our work as therapists, we have seen that ex-spouses sometimes move back in with the family for a short time to help the children practically and emotionally. Be aware that, if you decide to do this, your children might believe that it means you and your ex will reconcile. If this is an unrealistic expectation, explain clearly to your children what the situation is, how long you expect your ex to be with you, and what it means for their future.

Be careful about making major decisions during this time of stress and upheaval; this includes any decisions about reconciliation. Your feelings toward your ex-spouse may very well become clouded by nostalgia for former times and by the emotions that surround your illness, and it is important to move slowly and deliberately when considering any significant, life-altering choices.

When You Are Widowed

If you are a single parent because your partner has died, your illness may reignite and intensify unresolved grief. It is perfectly normal to feel angry about all of the losses in your life—including now the loss of your health—and to think that your situation is unfair. The sadness and pain over the loss of your partner may be increased by having to face your illness alone. During times of great joy or sorrow we miss our deceased family members most.

You may be afraid that your child will be left parentless. William, a widowed father, said,

> *I already have such a terrible sadness for my son that he lost his mother at such an early age. I don't know how he would survive losing both of his parents. I worry about it constantly and try to spend as much time as I possibly can either with him or writing letters to him. I know my prognosis is good, but I still feel like even the most remote possibility that I would die is heartbreaking.*

Because the outcome of your illness is out of your control, the concern can be a terrible burden.

Your children may have similar fears of being parentless, and their concerns about your illness may trigger intensely painful memories about the death of their other parent. Invite your children to share their concerns, normalize their reactions, and reassure them that you are doing all that you can to get well. Anticipate and address their concerns. Tell them, "I'm guessing you might be worried about who will take care of you if I have to be hospitalized." Explain what your plan is if that should happen. If you and your child are grieving in addition to coping with your illness, you may need to be more proactive about seeking alternate sources for emotional support and guidance. Ask a friend or family member to keep a close eye on your child and to tell you if he/she notices any signs of distress that you might miss. Finally, even though it can be frightening to talk about, many children ultimately feel reassured when their parents let them know that they have their affairs in order, including wills, living wills, and backup plans for guardianship. (The previous chapter explores these issues in more detail.) Share a basic outline of these details with your child.

Finding Support

If you cannot turn to your ex during this time of need, consider other supportive people who may help, including family members, former in-laws, friends, grandparents, and neighbors. Talk with your child's school counselors or teachers about what resources exist in the school system. Consult a social worker or your clergy for community resources or programs to help families in crisis.

Even if your ex is no longer a part of your life, your former in-laws may want to be involved but may be unsure of their roles. If you want them to help, consider making the first move and ask them if they would like to be involved. If they seem willing, make specific suggestions, such as babysitting, carpooling, or financial aid (tuition, assistance with health care, home care, housekeepers, or other expenses). You might ask them simply to visit more frequently to give your child the extra love and attention she needs. You might want to say something like, "I'm really tired and weak right now, and it's hard for me to play with Emily and give her the attention she needs. Would you be willing to come over on weekends and play with her and read to her?" Often, people will be grateful to be given a specific task so they know how they can help you most.

Dos and Don'ts for Going It Alone

- *Do* let people know what they can do to help you—and be specific.

- *Don't* neglect yourself or hold everything inside in an effort to be strong and take care of everyone else.

- *Do* remind yourself repeatedly that you are going through a crisis and you deserve help.

- *Do* find someone you trust to talk to about your feelings and experiences.

- *Do* prepare a list of emergency information such as family names and phone numbers, medical information, and names and phone numbers of your doctors.

- *Do* make a plan detailing with whom you want your children to stay if you are too ill to take care of them for a while.

- *Do* seek a way to communicate peacefully with your ex-spouse if you are divorced; if at all possible, consider writing a letter or extending an olive branch by inviting him or her to coffee or a meal.

- *Don't* make hasty decisions, such as reconciling with your ex.

- *Do* explain to your children what is going on. If you are divorced and your ex-spouse is around to help, explain that it does not mean that you are going to reconcile.

- *Do* acknowledge that your illness may well rekindle old pain, particularly if you are widowed.

- *Do* let caring people help with day-to-day needs like housework, cooking, and errands.

- *Do* talk to professionals such as school counselors, teachers, hospital social workers, or doctors to find out what resources are available for you and your children.

- ***Do*** understand that your former in-laws can possibly play a positive role in your healing, and your children might benefit from spending more time with them.

3. This Chapter Is for Partners

Up until now, the "you" we have been addressing is the person with the illness. In this chapter, though, the "you" we are talking to is that person's partner. If your loved one is seriously ill, you are bound to be affected on many different levels. Chances are good that you will have to deal with a lot more than the hardship of seeing your loved one suffer. You may be faced with the terrible difficulty of trying to help your partner care for himself and make medical decisions while at the same time trying to maintain a sense of balance in your own and your children's lives. For most people, it's hard to do all of that and still remain healthy, productive, and optimistic. Even the most conscientious, even-tempered, and organized of parents will struggle through this time.

One father we spoke with told us,

> *I am still trying to deal with my son's anger about how I handled things when my wife was sick—and she's been better for over five years. I was so worried about her, and sometimes when I'm afraid I act angry. I yelled at her, and at one point, I told her she wasn't even trying to get better. I tried to take care of everything, but I couldn't do it all, or at least I didn't do it very well. I'm still upset with myself for how I dealt with things, so I really don't blame my son for being angry with me, too.*

This man's daughter, now twenty, has a different take on how her father handled things:

I saw the big picture of everything that had to get done and how stressful it all was. It would have been pretty strange if my dad didn't sometimes lose it with all the pressure he was under trying to keep his career on track, cook and clean for us, drive us to school, and, on top of that, care for my mom, change her sheets, and clean up her vomit when she was really sick. He did get frustrated at times, but when she fell down and broke her arm she called for him, not for me, my brother, or my aunt who was also there. I think it was also easier for me to understand how he was feeling and what he was going through, because he has always communicated much more openly with me about his feelings than he has with my brother.

Though the upheaval created by a loved one's illness is multidimensional, it's possible that you and your family can weather this crisis and come out even stronger and closer than you were before. One woman told us,

At night, my husband stayed up to be in charge of my medicine. I didn't have to worry about it because he kept track of everything. And when my hair fell out, I remember going into the bedroom yelling. He was asleep, but he just woke up and comforted me. The whole experience just made us even closer. It really helped to know that, if there was anything I couldn't do, he was there to take care of it.

Even if the medical crisis does have the benefit of bringing you closer to your partner, that does not mean that it's going to be easy, or that you aren't going to have moments of confusion, resentment, or anger. It's important to be able to forgive yourself if your anger or sadness gets the best of you, and then to move on. Although your new role in your family may be challenging and at times frustrating, it is likely to be temporary. It will, though, have lingering effects, and there are many things you can do to ensure that those effects will be mainly positive ones.

Taking Care of Your Own Needs

Most people can't even imagine how devastating it can be to watch a loved one battle with a potentially deadly disease. It is painful to see the fear and uncertainty in your partner as he struggles to fight and control his illness. You will almost certainly worry that he might die, even if his prognosis is good. You may also feel unprepared to handle the realities of the illness since nothing can really prepare you for all of the changes you will face.

You may find yourself worrying about your own health and about what the future holds for you and your children. You may begin to wonder if you will be able to hold it all together. Also, during this peak time of stress, you may not have many people to talk to about your fears, particularly if you're used to turning to your partner in times of need. Many people feel a wide range of powerful emotions and, at the same time, a powerful need to protect their family members from the intensity of these emotions. Appearing strong and optimistic can be a real challenge at a time when your children and your partner need you most.

Remember that you can't take care of the rest of your family if you neglect yourself. Staying healthy means dealing with the emotional toll your partner's illness is taking on you. Most people try to deny the negative feelings they have, either because of guilt or because of a need to put up a good front. The wife of a man with multiple sclerosis told us,

You wonder, am I supposed to feel like this? I'm not supposed to be pissed. But because my husband is sick, we won't be able to take trips and take long walks anymore. I was really hard on myself for being angry until I realized those feelings were part of the process. It's alright to have feelings, and we should be aware of them. This illness has affected me in many ways, and my emotions are perfectly normal and okay.

Another woman, whose husband has cancer, told us how she finally figured out that she needed to deal with her emotions.

I felt like I had to put all of my emotions on the back-burner, to be strong for my husband and the kids. Suddenly, though, it all started taking over—the fear, the worry, the resentment—and I didn't know how to stop it. I finally went to a psychologist who told me it was okay to cry. I realized I had to pull down the walls I'd erected around myself and let people see what was really going on with me. That helped me.

In addition to trying to quell their emotions, many people also neglect their physical health. This neglect is understandable; most of us do that from time to time when we are stressed out, overworked, and anxious. We might turn to "quick fixes" for acute stress such as alcohol, stimulants, junk food, or cigarettes. It's easy to forget that when we feel the worst we need to take care of ourselves the most. Remember that it's crucial to carve out time to relax, stay fit, and have fun.

If you're a regular at the gym, make it a priority to continue going, even if you can go only twice a week instead of daily. If you notice that you are tense, consider treating yourself to a professional massage, even if you've never done that before. If you are a member of a social group, don't resign, even if you can't go to meetings as often as you did before.

Keeping yourself mentally and physically healthy does much more than just give you the strength to take care of your family. It also models for your children how they should take care of themselves and helps allay fears they may have about your health. In fact, it's a good idea to get regular medical check-ups and report the results to your children. For younger children, you might say, "I went to the doctor today, and I'm very healthy!" For older children and teens, you might give more specific details about what the doctor said. If the news is bad, don't hide that from your child, but try to be upbeat, and tell him what you're doing to fix the problem and take care of yourself.

Dealing with Increased Responsibilities

As you adjust to your partner's illness and the changes it creates in your family, you may find that you must take on new responsibilities. Judith had never done her family's taxes before her husband became seriously ill.

> *All of a sudden April 15 was approaching, and my husband was in a hospital in another state where he could get the best care. He was too sick to help me, even to tell me where I could find receipts and things and which forms to use. On top of that, I was trying to work, take trips to visit him, and help my son have as normal a childhood as possible. If my parents hadn't been such ready and willing babysitters, I don't think I could have made it. I took all the paperwork I could find and went to H&R Block. It got taken care of, but I felt like a helpless idiot.*

We frequently hear that partners of sick people feel exhausted, inadequate, and overwhelmed. The wife of a man with multiple sclerosis said, "You're just going along with your life, trying to get everything done, and suddenly you realize, 'I'm the powerful one in this family now. I'm the one who has to keep everything going.'" Keeping everything going can seem like an impossible task, particularly if your partner has responsibilities that you have never taken on before.

One man whose wife had cancer told us,

> *I didn't mind giving my wife injections or cleaning up after her when she was sick. I didn't mind driving the kids to school and picking them up. The main thing that drove me crazy at first was going to the grocery store. That was always her job, and for some reason walking down those aisles by myself always brought home to me the fact that she was too sick to do this. It made me feel very alone.*

It's sometimes the little things that sneak up on you that suddenly seem colossal.

If your partner was the one who always paid the bills, it might seem daunting to take that on. If she always drove your grandmother to her card game on Tuesday afternoon, you might have to start doing that. One option, though, is to enlist the help of others, whether friends and family or professionals. There might be someone else who wouldn't mind taking grandmother to her card game on Tuesday afternoon. Many people believe they have to do it all alone, but that is rarely the case.

Sometimes people need to travel for their medical care. If you need to accompany your partner on such trips, consider who should take care of your children and pets during that time. Think about who would be available, willing, and able to provide the most consistent routines for your children. Who would your child feel most safe and comfortable with? Even if you are not currently travelling, plan for that possibility by making tentative arrangements in advance with potential childcare providers. Let your children know that they will be cared for in the event of any parental absences.

Make plans with your partner for changes in the normal routine due to travel for treatments. Make a list of the things he normally does that you need to take care of when he receives treatments or has surgery. If you don't know how to do something, perhaps he or someone else can talk you through it. Consider having your bank automatically pay recurring bills (such as mortgage or rent, credit cards, telephone, utilities, cable, etc.). If you usually cook and your partner does the dishes, your teenager can learn to do one or the other to help out.

Simplify your life wherever possible. Sit down and figure out what can be done to make life easier for you and your family during this difficult time. Should your daughter be allowed to quit the tennis lessons she's never really liked? Can you afford to hire a fulltime babysitter or a housekeeper once a week? Can a friend help your children with their homework or drive them to school? Say "yes" when someone asks, "Is there anything I can do to help?" Right there on the spot, figure out how they can be helpful, whether by babysitting, bringing your family a home-cooked meal, or going to lunch with you so you can have a little cheerful companionship. Not only will you and your family benefit from your acceptance of their help, but your friends and family will be happier and feel less helpless knowing that they are contributing to your welfare.

Keeping Informed about Your Partner's Illness

For many people, the most difficult part of a loved one's illness is their inability to fix it. When we care about each other, we want to take care of each other, and a loved one's illness is something we have very little control over. Remember that loving and caring for someone is different from having control over their life. Bob, whose partner has AIDS, told us, "You think you have control over your life, and then something like this happens. I can't control my partner's illness. I can't stop it or start it. People say to try different things, and we do, but we're always just reacting to it, not controlling it." Remind yourself repeatedly that you can still do a lot, even if you can't fix the problem.

Perhaps the best way to deal with the frustration of having so little control is to stay informed about your partner's illness, prognosis, and treatment options. Go to the doctor with him, if he agrees. Contact organizations dedicated to the illness, such as the American Cancer Society, to ask about newsletters and other sources of information and support. Read books about your partner's illness or do research on the Internet. Go to any search engine such as Google or Yahoo, and you will find a wealth of potential contacts. Just remember that you shouldn't believe everything you read. Many Internet chat rooms, for example, have an overabundance of half-baked advice and misinformation. Make sure the websites you visit are reputable, and check out questionable information with a doctor. (Chapter 6 provides more tips on the pros and cons of using the Internet and social media.)

Information is power. Having it can give you a sense of control to help counteract the inevitable powerlessness people feel when a loved one is in danger. Accurate information can assist you in helping your partner make intelligent decisions. It can also help you explain to your children the medical aspects of their parent's illness.

Keeping the Relationship Healthy

No matter how limited your ability to keep your partner healthy, you can do a lot to keep your relationship healthy, and that may now be more important than ever. Serious illnesses disrupt social lives and could cause you to neglect special occasions like anniversaries and birthdays.

Keep a calendar with anniversaries, birthdays, and other special days marked on it, and find ways to celebrate those occasions with your partner, even if only by sharing a special dinner in your hospital room. If you and your partner went on regular dates when she was well, find ways to continue those dates, even if it's in a revised form. The children can be watched by a babysitter even if the two of you are just spending some time alone in another room, talking or watching a movie.

Be prepared for changes in your sexual relationship. Due to her illness, your partner may not feel attractive or interested in sex, and she may be too ill to desire any physical contact. You may also feel disinterested in sex or lack attraction to your partner. Many partners worry that they are being selfish if they have sexual needs during this time. It's not selfish; it's perfectly normal. You will want to keep in mind, though, that these feelings must be secondary to your partner's recovery and try not to be critical if your partner is unable to have sex with you. Remind yourself that the situation will likely improve when your partner recovers.

Take time to communicate. Don't try to anticipate what your partner will need; spend time asking her. It's normal to get worn down and consequently to become less communicative when someone you love is ill. Set aside some time to talk about your day, the highs and the lows. Include your partner in the life you lead away from her sickbed. Make sure to inform her about your children's schoolwork, sports events, projects, and social lives, and to consult her concerning decisions about them. You may have to make more of an effort to communicate about these issues than you did before she was sick if she is not able to attend events like school plays or dance recitals.

If Your Relationship Is Already Rocky

The stress of facing a serious illness puts added pressure on a relationship, particularly if it is already on shaky ground. Some couples find that facing a life-threatening illness brings them closer by putting their problems in new perspective, while others find that it only deepens the pre-existing cracks in the relationship. Even though your partner is sick, don't lose sight of the fact that your own needs are important, too. Be especially careful, though, about making any major life decisions, like separating or divorcing. One mother whose ex-husband was hospitalized says, "It didn't matter that he and I were not on good terms; at the end of the day, he's my children's father. I just had to be there for him during that time because it was what my kids needed me to do."

Communicating with Your Children

As the healthy parent, you may be the one who deals with your children's feelings most of the time. The way your child reacts will be highly individual. Most children show incredible empathy, patience, and concern when a parent is ill, but it is never easy for them. No doubt your children will feel frightened and will, at some point, act out in anger or revert to an earlier stage of development. Whether they show it or not, they will be particularly worried during extended hospital stays, surgeries, and painful treatments. They may be shocked or disgusted if your partner's illness causes noticeable changes in her physical appearance. They may also resent any added responsibilities the illness brings or major changes in their schedules.

Your child may express his sadness by directing his anger at you. Some children lash out at their healthy parent because it feels safer than venting their rage on themselves, their sick parent, or the world. Their anger may be a call for help, letting you know that they are hurting. It may also serve to help them release pent up feelings that they are not aware of. While you want to be sensitive to your child's feelings, you should also be clear about setting limits. For example, you might say, "I know that Daddy's being sick is very hard on you, and you're probably very sad and angry that he got sick and that so much in our lives has changed. But it's not okay for you to call me names or to hit me. Let's talk about what's going on and find some other ways that you can express your feelings."

Your children will benefit from your willingness to reveal how you feel about your partner's illness. If you are open about your own emotions and vulnerability, they will be more free to express their own sentiments. Many people believe it's too frightening for children to see a parent cry or hear a parent express helplessness. While it is true that your child will become anxious if you completely fall apart in front of him, tears are not something you need to hide. If you cry as you reveal your concerns about your partner to your child, you can explain, "I'm crying because I'm sad that Mommy is so sick." Preteens and teens probably won't need any explanation.

When sharing information with your children, show that you respect their opinions but that you do not expect them to be responsible for major decisions regarding their parent's care. Sarah, a teenager whose mom had cancer, told us,

> *My father told me we couldn't take care of my mom at home anymore and asked me to research which nursing home would be best for her. Eventually, it became really hard for me to spend time with my friends. They were worried about who would ask them to prom, and I was worried about which nursing home I should put my mother in.*

Some teens might appreciate doing some research; it can be empowering for them to know that they can help. Explain that, while their help is greatly appreciated, you will be making the final decisions. Feel your child out to learn whether helping out in that way is okay with him. Children can handle unpleasant details about illness, but they are not mature enough to shoulder major decisions about medical care or nursing homes that have serious emotional and practical consequences for the family.

Retain some structure and routine in your family life. Children need consistency, particularly when other aspects of family life are uncertain. As much as possible, don't let your children neglect important things, like schoolwork. Be flexible, though, and be prepared for things to fall apart at times. Let your children know that you are bound to make mistakes when performing tasks that are normally your partner's responsibility. Ask them to help you by reminding you what things are most important to them. They can assist you in prioritizing by telling you that they would rather have you attend a school play than every soccer practice. Finally, make time to have fun with them, even if it means skipping doing the dishes or missing a piano practice.

Staying Connected

It is natural for you occasionally to want to bury your head in the sand and not deal with anyone outside of the immediate family. It's okay to let voicemail shield you for a while, but be sure to return those caring calls when you feel up to it. Answering the same questions over and over again about your partner's health can be annoying and exhausting, even when you appreciate the sympathy and good intentions of the inquirer. A key element in getting families through an illness, though, is often the support of their communities, including extended family, friends, religious groups, and neighbors. Keep in touch with email updates to the people who care.

A teenager whose mother had a brain tumor described the impact of community on her family. Reflecting on the first time her mother had surgery, she said,

I was shocked that my father expected us to keep going to church every Sunday through her long recovery. I was so scared for my mom and sort of angry at the world. I felt like no one could understand. The women at church brought us casseroles every night, and I thought that just symbolized how little anyone could do to help us. Now my mom is recovering from her third surgery, and my opinion has changed. You think a casserole might not mean a lot, but really it means everything to me. It means that people are out there thinking about my family and caring about us.

An Unexpected Miracle: Learning and Growing Through Adversity

Many families report that there is an upside that comes with the crisis of illness. Friends and family members come together, help each other out, and grow closer than they would ever have been had they not faced such adversity. If this upside happens in your family, relish those moments, record them in a letter or journal, talk about them with your children, and try not to be too disappointed when they don't last. It will probably be your responsibility to highlight these moments for others in your family. Chances are good that your partner will feel too sick to really appreciate them when they are happening, and your children may not have the life experience to recognize them for what they are until later. Through the inevitable ups and downs, what your family learns about each other will last a lifetime.

People who have been through the crisis of caring for a seriously ill family member report that they somehow found the strength to accomplish things they never felt possible. Amy, who worked fulltime and cared for three children throughout her husband's debilitating degenerative illness, said, "I took the bull by the horns because I didn't have any choice in the matter. I realized that I was stronger than I thought I was." While feeling terrified inside, she knew she had to keep herself together to take care of her children and husband. A father of two told us, "My kids really kept me going because my wife went into such a depression that I had no choice but to keep going. It makes you look at life completely differently. It opened my eyes and made me appreciate what I had around me." As much as possible, remember to appreciate any small blessings or life lessons that come as a result of your family's crisis.

Dos and Don'ts for the Partner

- *Don't* quit taking care of yourself. You and your family will benefit if you continue to perform those activities that help you relax and feel good about yourself.

- *Don't* be too hard on yourself if you "lose it" every now and then. Expressing your anger can sometimes clear the air and clarify everyone's feelings.

- *Do* talk to your partner about how you feel about her illness if you feel she is strong enough to discuss it with you.

- *Do* tell yourself frequently that you're doing the job of two people and at the same time coping with the crisis of your partner's illness.

- *Do* ask your partner about his routines and responsibilities. Ask him what things he normally does that you need to take over, and make sure you have a clear understanding of how to do them.

- *Don't* try to handle everything on your own. Enlist the help of experts and loved ones.

- *Do* keep informed about your partner's illness by talking with her doctor, reading books, or researching online.

- *Don't* forget special occasions, like anniversaries. Put them on a calendar or have your smartphone send you reminders.

- *Do* be creative about how to celebrate special occasions. What matters is that you celebrate in the right spirit, not how fancy the restaurant you go to is.

- *Do* continue to have dates or special "outings" with your partner, even if these are conducted in your bedroom or even a hospital room.

- *Do* set aside time to communicate with your partner about your own and your children's lives—past, present, and future.

- *Do* talk to your children about how you're feeling and how they're feeling.

- *Don't* pressure your children to help you make major life decisions or cope with strong emotions.

- *Do* be flexible, but *don't* let the structure fall apart in your family.

- *Do* remember to tell your children you love them, and make time to do fun things with them.

- *Don't* isolate yourself from the people who care about you.

- *Do* continue attending church, synagogue, neighborhood association meetings, reading groups, clubs, or any other organizations that keep you connected to a wider community.

- *Do* turn off the phone when you need a break from the outside world, as long as you turn it back on again when you're ready.

- *Do* send emails updating everyone on your partner's prognosis, so that you can keep others informed without having to answer the same questions over and over.

- *Do* make a point of thanking your children when they're cooperative, helpful, or empathic.

- *Do* talk to your family members about what you all are learning and how you all are growing closer as a result of this family crisis.

- *Do* record your thoughts in a journal, so your family can remember later how you all came together and got closer.

- *Don't* expect moments of closeness and cooperation to last forever. Don't be too angry or disappointed when they end. There will be others.

Being Kept in the Dark

Kelly's Story

Kelly was thirteen when her mother was diagnosed with leukemia. Throughout the weeks of testing prior to the diagnosis, Kelly was never informed that something could be wrong. Her mother was already in the hospital when her father told her, "Your mom has leukemia."

Unfortunately, he didn't explain to Kelly what leukemia was or what it might mean for her mother and their family. She looked in the encyclopedia, but the medical information she found there did not answer her personal, emotional questions. Kelly reports, "I didn't ask questions because that wasn't what we were brought up to do in my family. But it would have been so much better if it could have been explained to me by someone who loved me."

During her mother's long hospitalization, Kelly visited nightly. On her first visit, she asked the doctor if her mother was going to die, and he told her she wasn't. She was never allowed to talk to the doctor again, and she was never told that her mother's condition was worsening.

When her mother went to another state for treatment, her parents sent her to stay with family friends while her older brother moved in with a school friend. "They pretty much abandoned me," Kelly says. She struggled with insecurity as a teenager in a new school, with new friends and no family or support system in place. Needless to say, she felt isolated and alone. Fortunately, a school counselor and a kind teacher provided nurturing and support.

Though her father reported daily on her mother's blood count, Kelly never understood the meaning of those numbers. No one ever asked her how she felt, so she got the message that she was not supposed to talk about her feelings or express her needs.

Her mother eventually returned home, but Kelly remained with the other family throughout her mother's frequent hospitalizations. On the day her mother died, Kelly had just come home from a football game. The woman she was staying with told her that they were going to the hospital to visit her mother and that she should bring Kleenex. She was too surprised to ask why, but did as she was told. At the hospital, her mother looked "out of it" and was hooked to many machines. Kelly sat on the hospital bed and told her mother about the football game. That's the last thing time she talked to her mother. Minutes later, with Kelly out of the room, her mother died.

Kelly never said goodbye or told her mother she loved her. She never knew her mother was dying. Not only had the doctor clearly told her months earlier that her mother would live, but no one had ever told her anything different since. Kelly later learned that her father had signed a "do not resuscitate" order for her mother, but he had not told Kelly. Nearly a decade later, Kelly is still angry and wonders what she would have done differently had she known her mother was going to die.

Kelly wonders still why she wasn't told her mother was dying, so she could exchange some last words with her.

She wonders why her mother chose not to say goodbye to her or leave any specially prepared messages for her. She says, "I'll always look for the letter that she never wrote. I hoped when I graduated high school and college and when I got married that there would be something from her. I can't imagine that somebody would know she was dying, and never say anything to her child."

Kelly hopes that other parents will learn from her story. "Talk to your kids no matter what," she says. "Let them know that they can come to you with their questions and feelings. My parents assumed that I knew more than I did. Don't do that with your kids. Talk to them every day, even if they seem okay on the outside."

4. The Effect on Children of All Ages

If you have received the diagnosis of a serious illness, tell your children as soon as possible. The first thing to figure out is when and how to break this news to them. Many parents wait a while, fearing their children's reactions or their own. It's normal to need some time to absorb the shock before you make any important decisions about how to communicate the news to your children, but you can't put it off for too long because children can be very perceptive when something is seriously wrong with a parent.

Rebecca, a mother of three, recalls how difficult telling her children about her illness was.

We put off telling the kids for several weeks, mainly because we were on a fact-finding mission to find out an exact prognosis and to determine what kind of treatment I would need. Based on my biopsy and my treatment plan, I knew I was going to have chemo and lose my hair. I realized I was going to look really sick, almost like I was dying. I needed to let my kids know that I was sick but also that I was fighting this, and I was not dying. It never occurred to me that they might think they caused me to get sick, but that's how a child's mind works. They internalize everything. They think, "This is my fault because I didn't make my bed, or I was sassy to my mom" or whatever else. So, I knew I had to tell them what was going on, but that day that I told them, that was a horrible day.

Talk to your partner or a trusted friend to come up with some ideas about how best to deliver the news to the children. You may also want to meet with your doctor for advice about explaining the details of your illness in a way that children can understand. Your doctor may also be willing to meet with your family, which can be useful if the medical details are baffling or new to you, and you don't have the answers to your family's questions.

While it's perfectly all right to take time to get your emotions in check and your information in order, we strongly recommend that you tell your children what's going on as soon as possible. Don't do what some parents do and convince yourself that the children don't need to know or that you will get better before they know what's going on. Also, don't assume that your children are too young to understand and that telling them will only frighten or worry them, which actually is an approach some doctors (mistakenly) recommend. While you certainly want to evaluate the age and maturity level of your child (see Chapter 5), all children recognize stress in their parents and respond to it. As Harriet Lerner states in *The Mother Dance* (Harper Collins, 1998, 147), "If our kids can't trust us to tell them the truth about issues that affect them, they have difficulty trusting the universe, including their internal universe of thoughts, feelings, and perceptions." As Kelly learned, there was no way for her mother to restore that trust once she was gone.

It's common to fret over choosing the right time or place or words to describe the situation. Said one parent of talking to her children, "I felt like I couldn't come up with the answers quickly enough because I was trying to deal with my own anxiety and my own sadness. The picture became too broad." Other parents wait, hoping someone else will tell their children for them, but it is almost always better for them to hear difficult news from you.

Furthermore, your children may resent you later if they think that you are neglecting this responsibility. A young woman whose mother survived cancer recalls,

> *My high school graduation was the night before her first surgery. After graduation, I drove to New Orleans for the night with a group of friends. When I got home my father met me at the door. He told me that my mom had been diagnosed with breast cancer, and she was waiting upstairs to speak to me. She would leave for the hospital the next morning at 5 A.M. I felt dizzy and scared as I walked up the stairs to my mother. She was tucked in bed, crying. I recall having very mixed feelings about their choice to tell me the night before her extended stay in the hospital. I understood they wanted me to enjoy the graduation with my friends, but it felt so strange that such important information had been withheld, and I felt so unprepared for what was to come over the next several months. As I began to reflect, I was frustrated with myself that their stress, intensity, and distance over the previous weeks had not served as a warning sign that something was wrong.*

One reason parents may find it difficult to tell their children about their illness is that they fear they themselves will break down or look weak. Parents should consider their own ability to cope with their child's reactions, whatever they may be. Remember, it is perfectly healthy and appropriate to cry when discussing the seriousness of your illness. Your children may benefit from seeing how you cope with your own feelings and will feel safer about expressing their own reactions when you set this example.

Don't be afraid to talk about your own emotions, and ask your partner to do the same. Most parents are not very good at hiding strong emotions from their children, so your child will probably be aware that something is amiss. If you don't have a handle on your own feelings, it will be extremely difficult to talk openly and honestly with your children.

We suggest writing down ideas that you want to share in advance, and practicing with a partner, friend, or counselor to help you become more comfortable with talking about these painful issues. Hearing yourself say these things out loud for the first time may shock you, but practicing may help lessen the force of your emotions.

Getting the Message Across

Telling your child that you are ill might be the most difficult discussion you have had with her, so you will want to be as prepared as possible. Keep in mind, though, that you have a lot of experience communicating with your child, so you already know a lot about how she likes to be told things and what sort of questions she is likely to ask. Your experience as a parent will kick in to help you find the approach you need.

Here are a few suggestions about how you might get your message across in a clear and non-threatening manner:

- *Use simple, direct language.* No matter what age, your child will likely feel confused and frightened, so it is important to be as clear as possible. Provide detailed, concrete information to explain that you are sick. Say what your illness is called and what your treatment will probably look like.

- *Spend time alone with each child.* If you have more than one child, you might tell them all at the same time. If you do that, make sure you subsequently spend some time alone with each child to address their unique reactions and questions.

- *Don't censor emotions.* Tell your children that you expect them to have many feelings, including anger, sadness, and confusion about the changes your illness will mean for them. Let them know that it's okay for them to share their feelings, even the negative ones. If you aren't strong enough to discuss your children's feelings with them, suggest another adult with whom they can talk when they are upset.

- *Don't try quick fixes.* Children often perceive efforts to soothe their anxieties with a quick "Don't worry about it" as dismissing or rejecting their feelings. It's better to validate these by acknowledging that your child must be scared, and allowing her to talk about it. The words "sick," "illness," and "death" should not be avoided. We have found that children get angry when their parents speak about illness in hushed tones or euphemisms. Parents often think they are sparing their children, but avoidance often has the effect of scaring them even more.

- *Encourage and look for nonverbal communication.* Look for ways to help your child express her emotions nonverbally. Young children, in particular, express their feelings through nonverbal means more than adults, which is why their play is so significant. Don't stifle your child if she seems to play out angry themes. For example, don't tell her to, "Play nice, and stop killing all of your dolls." Watch her, and try to use her play as a springboard for discussions about how she's doing. Encourage her to express her feelings in drawings, and provide opportunities for her to let out her frustrations through physical activities such as sports or trips to the playground. With teens, you might suggest that they keep journals, write letters, either to you or to friends, and write short stories, poetry, songs, or comic strips to help them express what is going on. It may also help them to draw, exercise, or work with clay to release pent up emotions.

• *Provide prompt words and pictures.* Sometimes it helps to give young children (about five to eight years old) a list of "feeling words"—like mad, sad, aggravated, etc.— and to ask if any of these are true for them now. For a younger child, you might say, "Sometimes kids your age get angry or scared when a parent is sick. Do you feel either of those things?" Familiarize yourself with the common reactions for children of different ages that we explore in Chapter 5.

• *Give extra hugs and kisses.* Show extra affection and love for your child. Hug and kiss her, and tell her often that you love her and value what she has to say. Even older children may crave affection they have long since "grown out of." A teenager might want to hold your hand, sit on your lap, or snuggle in bed. Don't rebuff any shows of affection on their part, but also don't force shows of affection on them.

- *Talk about physical changes you may go through.* Explain to your child how your appearance may change throughout the course of your treatment. For example, chemotherapy can cause hair loss or skin changes. Medication may cause you to gain or lose weight. If you might be hooked up to machines, tell your child what those will look like. Physical changes can be unsettling for children, especially if they have not been warned ahead of time about what to expect. As one mother said,

  > I remember tucking my son in one night, and he asked me if I was going to die. I remember thinking, "Oh my God, I must look so bad." I told him "I know I look like death walking, but the treatment that's causing me to look this way is also what's going to make me better." I kept reminding him that I was going to be okay, but I realized then that my words didn't match my appearance.

- *Discuss hospital visits.* If your child will be visiting you in the hospital, consider showing her a photo or video beforehand to educate her about what to expect and to explain the purpose of any medical apparatus. Preparing to see such equipment can protect children from their fear of the unknown. Talk about when you will be in the hospital, who will take them to visit you, and how often they might visit.

Try to stay as positive as possible, even though the topic is painful and scary. You might say, "I'm scared about my illness, too, but no matter how scared I get, I am still going to give it my very best shot and do everything I can to fight this disease and stay healthy." Even if your child denies being anxious or scared, she will be comforted when she recognizes that you are feeling the same way and that you understand her.

Even if you've talked to your children and addressed all of their questions and concerns, you may have to revisit the topic several times. This need to revisit the issue is especially true of young children. Don't assume that because your children act "normal" or don't ask questions that everything is okay, or that they aren't confused or forgetful about what you've tried to explain.

However you decide to communicate facts about your illness to your children, the most important factor is to be honest and to give them the information they need to understand and deal with the changes that will occur because of your illness. It's okay to say "I don't know" if your children ask you a question beyond your scope. Let them know that if you don't know the answer now, you'll find it out.

Maintaining Balance in Your Children's Lives

Naturally, family life will be unsettled from time to time throughout your illness. It is important for your children, though, that some things in their lives remain as normal as possible. Talk to them about what might change in their routines, and be clear about what you expect from them.

Remind your school-aged children and teens that their most important responsibility continues to be doing well in school. Explain to your younger children that you want them to continue to play and make friends, and tell your teens that they need to hang out with friends, even if they are worried about you.

Encourage your child to talk with her friends, and provide opportunities for your child to socialize. Let your child know that it is okay to share what is going on with others. If there are details that you prefer to keep private, be specific with your child about what is "private family business," with the understanding that anything not so designated can be shared with others.

Maintain discipline. Let your children know you are not going to quit disciplining them or setting limits when they do things wrong. Your ability to follow through with this important parenting job can, oddly enough, be reassuring to a child when there is a lot of confusion and chaos in her life.

If someone besides you will be taking care of your children during your illness, let them know who that will be and what they can expect. If your children's daily routine will change, let them know that this change is temporary and that you will resume your role as quickly as you can. Let them express discontent or worry about changes, and assure them that you are doing what you need to do to keep them safe and make daily tasks go as easily as possible for them.

If you will rely on your children to take care of themselves and to run the household more than you have in the past, make sure that their new roles are age-appropriate. For example, a sixteen-year-old might make dinner, while an eight-year-old could set the table. Children should not be expected to discipline one another, regardless of their ages. Doing so can lead to animosity and abuse of power. If you have questions about whether your child's responsibilities are age-appropriate, consult family members, counselors, or religious leaders.

Create rituals or simple jobs to make your children feel useful. One eleven-year-old girl whose mother was sick with cancer took over a task that she enjoyed and that also made her feel valued by her mother. Before her illness, her mother regularly visited a salon for weekly manicures and was proud of her nails. When she could no longer go because of her illness, she asked her daughter to help by bringing her the supplies she needed. Soon, a ritual developed, and they began giving themselves manicures once a week. Another mother said,

> *My kids wanted to do something, so I started to give them jobs like bringing me toast in the morning. When I was healing from surgery, they started calling themselves "the foot massage fairies," and they would come to me with lotions and towels, and they would rub my feet and hands. My five-year-old would say to me, "We're going to bring you the relaxation. Are you ready for the relaxation?" They banded together, and it was really sweet.*

Understanding Your Child's Reactions to Your Illness

A child's whole life changes when a parent develops a serious illness, and these changes can be profound even when they are temporary. Sometimes, these changes trigger emotions that adults might consider unacceptable. Children can resent their parent because the illness prevents them from being like the rest of their friends. One mother told us, "I was confused at first with how self-absorbed my seven-year-old was. She was really angry at me and upset that I was sick. She immediately expressed a lot of concern that she would never have a play date again. We had just moved to this town and I was ruining her life." Your children may appear totally indifferent to your suffering, but try not to take it personally. They are struggling to preserve themselves in the midst of a personal tragedy.

Children can tolerate painful and difficult information, often better than parents think they can. That doesn't mean they won't have feelings about it. Children may have a variety of responses to learning about their parent's illness. Some will want to be as close as possible to the sick parent. Children of all ages will experience sympathy for their sick parent and make serious efforts to help. Some children become very curious, asking many questions and wanting to see everything that happens. Some children become lonely and isolated, as if they are the only person in the world dealing with this issue. They may feel neglected by one or both parents who are focused on managing the illness. If your child responds in any of these ways, look into children's support groups. Or consider finding another child who has been through a similar situation who may be able to share their story. Such a common bond may make your child feel less alone. You might also seek an adult who has experienced a parent's illness when she was a child and would be willing to share that.

Children are comforted when parents and others treat them normally. Help them to maintain regular routines, including performing household chores, keeping up with schoolwork, and participating in the same social life as before. Parents should not, however, feel guilty about the sacrifices their children must inevitably make (for example, not being able to have friends visit when you are very ill).

Most children are reassured by knowledge, so it's important to be as honest and forthright as possible. Keeping lines of communication open with your children gives them a healthy example of how you can control the way you and your family respond to an illness even when you can't control the disease itself. For children and adults alike, not knowing what's going on is often more stressful than knowing the truth. Children of all ages will create their own stories to help them understand if they aren't given enough information about what concerns them. Unfortunately, with young children, these stories can often involve the child blaming herself for causing the illness. For example, a child who once accidentally hit her mother in the chest thought that she had caused her mother's breast cancer. Even if your child denies feeling at fault, be very clear that nothing they said, did, or didn't do made you sick. If your child is very young, you may have to repeat this often.

Older school-age children may feel compelled to master the illness intellectually. They may want to write school reports about the illness, research all the gory details, and try to assume caretaking duties for a sense of control. They may have difficulty articulating strong emotions, and they may act out rather than talking about their feelings. Although one eight-year-old child said she was coping well with her mother's illness, her parents noticed that she had begun eating compulsively and gaining a great deal of weight.

Teenagers will likely express a wide variety of fluctuating emotions and needs. Young teens, especially, waver between dependence on and independence from the ill parent, which can be confusing for everyone. In general, adolescent boys tend to distance themselves from the sick parent while adolescent girls tend to remain close to that parent while at the same time pursuing relationships with peers and love interests.

Respect your child's need for privacy. She may need time alone to deal with her feelings, especially when she is upset. For preteens and young teens, grief is usually very private. However, private time should not be allowed to turn into withdrawal, which is prolonged and sustained and could indicate problems coping with stress. If your teen no longer spends time socializing with friends or family, talk to her about it directly. If this withdrawal goes on for a month or longer, consider seeking professional help.

Younger children might worry that they, or the other parent, will catch what you have. Misconceptions like these can instigate guilt, anger, and fear. Most parents will want to do the right thing, but sometimes it is hard to know what the right thing is. The best approach is to "seize the moment." When something comes up—if your hair begins to fall out, for example—explain to your child what's going on. One mother addressed her daughter's fear about her mother's hair loss by letting her daughter help cut her hair when it began to fall out. Being included gave the girl a sense that she had some things under control and helped her to manage her feelings about seeing her mother with no hair.

Some children may become frightened or even repulsed by the illness or by certain treatments and physical changes. Though this can be unsettling, it is a normal reaction. Your children may back away or withdraw from you or even act as if you don't exist. A toddler might start crying and refuse to be held by you if she is frightened by a change in your appearance. Usually you can work through this problem by addressing the issue head on. You might say, "I know I look different and that can be scary, but I'm still Mommy and I love you." One mother with leukemia said her young son was disgusted by the smell caused by the chemotherapy and radiation treatments, and he did not want to go near her. Needless to say, his reaction was painful for his mother, and she had to work to overcome her hurt and reassure him that she was still the same person inside and that she loved him.

Another mother who lost her hair during chemo said,

The vanity component was a big issue for all of my kids. My middle child didn't want me to go to school events. There were times when I didn't want to put on a wig to go out to eat because it was hot, the chemo was making me hotter, and I was also having hot flashes. My kids would say, "You have to put the wig on," and I would say, "Then we're not going out to eat." My husband was frustrated and didn't understand why we were all so hung up on the wig. He would say, "Get in the car. Your mom feels good enough to go out to eat, so we're going to take her out to eat."

Though you may be hurt, angry, sad, or frustrated by your child's reaction, she is not expressing feelings about you but rather about the illness and the changes it has caused in you and your family.

Pay attention to indirect communication from your children. Do they avoid eye contact with you? Do they avoid touching? It might help your child if, as you talk to her, you try to predict how she may be feeling. You might say, "I read how a little girl was very frightened when her mother's hair fell out because of chemotherapy. Do you worry about how I will look when that happens?"

Even the most insightful and sensitive parent who understands, intellectually, his child's reaction, may feel hurt by rejection. Try not to reject your child in return or to get angry. Give your child space to think about and get a grip on her feelings. Tell her you know you don't look or act the same. Remind her that you are doing what you can to get better. Tell her it's okay to be afraid or sad or angry, and remind her how much you love her.

Your children have the right to mourn the losses your illness has imposed on your family. They need to release their emotions, and you can help them find effective, non-destructive means to do so. One young boy was too angry and hurt to discuss his feelings for a long time, so he coped by being mean to everyone around him. His family took him to a therapist who, instead of trying to get him to talk before he was ready, gave him piles of paper and old magazines to rip up. He released negative energy in this way for several sessions before he was ready to start talking. Sometimes words just aren't sufficient to express our reactions to what we find terrible, and you are uniquely capable of helping your child find creative and constructive ways to get it all out.

If You Are Hospitalized

If you have to be hospitalized during your illness, your children may fear that you will never return home. If your illness requires a planned, extended hospital stay, take measures to set up a comfortable, supportive environment for your children while you are gone. Reassure your child that she will be taken care of. Tell her with whom she will be staying and when she will be able to come and see you. Let her know how long you expect to be in the hospital and why you are going in. If you are too sick to discuss these matters with your child, ask your partner or a close relative or friend to do it for you. Talk to teachers, counselors, or other school officials who can provide emotional support and be on the lookout for changes in your child's mood or behavior.

If there is a possibility that you will have an emergency hospitalization (and that is always possible when someone is ill), make sure you have a plan for how your family will deal with that, and let your child know what that plan is. Don't worry that you might scare her by introducing the idea that such an emergency might occur. Preparing for that scare would be nothing compared to the panic she would feel if you were suddenly hospitalized and she was clueless about plans for her continued care.

Find ways to communicate regularly with your child during your stay in the hospital, even if she can't visit you every day. Coordinate regular telephone times or send daily emails. One mother who was so ill that her children were not allowed to visit her in the hospital noted,

> *I was like the girl in the bubble for about a week because my white blood cells were so low. My children weren't allowed in my room, and even the medical personnel had to wear masks and gloves and had to wash in and out. It was hard, but I communicated daily with my kids using FaceTime, so I was able to see them even if I couldn't be with them.*

Many parents also write letters or send text messages or videos. If your child is not old enough to read or write, you can ask her to draw pictures to decorate your hospital room.

Give your child some personal item of yours to keep with her while you are away to help her feel connected to you, such as clothing, jewelry, or a photo. Ask her if she would be willing to give you something of hers to take with you as well, such as a favorite stuffed animal, a book, or a photo. Discuss these and other ideas with your child, encouraging her to come up with her own ideas about what would make your hospitalization easier for her.

Dos and Don'ts for the Effect on Children of All Ages

- *Do* talk with someone you trust to come up with ideas for how to share the news with your child.

- *Do* consider asking your doctor to meet with you and your child to explain your treatment.

- *Do* tell your children about your illness as soon as possible.

- *Do* think about practicing with a friend or family member before talking with your child. Also, consider writing down what you might say.

- *Don't* try to hide your feelings when talking with your child. It's okay to cry.

- *Do* recognize that your child may resent having her life change as a result of your illness.

- *Do* remember that children will have a variety of responses to learning about your illness. There is no "right" way for a child to feel about a parent's illness.

- *Do* maintain routines in the family as much as possible.

- *Don't* push your child to talk if she doesn't want to.

- *Do* assure your child that she has not done anything to cause your illness.

- *Do* try to help your child find safe and healthy ways to express her feelings.

- *Do* keep your child's school informed about what's going on so teachers or counselors can provide support and be on the lookout for changes in your child's mood or behavior.

- *Do* let your child know what to expect if you have a hospitalization planned, including details about with whom she will be staying and how long you will be gone.

- *Don't* assume that your family will work out a plan if you have to be hospitalized in an emergency. Make plans ahead of time.

- *Do* communicate with your child from the hospital, and have her visit often if possible.

- *Do* give your children something personal of yours to keep with them while you are hospitalized to help them feel connected to you.

5. Getting Them Through It
~ Children of All Ages ~

L ike most parents, you want more than anything to protect your children from suffering. During a family crisis this instinct to protect may lead you to assume that your children can't really understand what's going on, so they don't need to know. This assumption would likely be more a product of your own hopes and fears than what is real for your child. Children of all ages can understand something about what is happening when a parent is not available to take care of them as before. What you should tell your children about your illness depends on their ages and maturity levels. The way children respond to what you tell them, and to the changes brought about by your illness, depends both on the individual child and on his stage of development.

In this chapter we discuss how children typically react to a parent's illness according to their developmental stages, and we offer suggestions for helping them cope with the feelings they have about your illness. You may notice the same reactions described in different stages; this is because there is often a lot of overlap in the way children react, and the differences between levels of development can be subtle.

There is a wide range of "normal" reactions to a parent's illness, but just because a reaction is normal doesn't always mean it's acceptable. Sometimes children develop behavior problems when they are feeling sad, frightened, or frustrated. It might help for you to first acknowledge that your child's reaction is understandable before explaining to him that certain behaviors are unacceptable. Your goal should be to help your child move from "acting out" to "acting on" his emotions.

No matter what his age, your child will need both your emotional support and your discipline. When you are ill, you may feel too exhausted to enforce limits or too guilty to mete out punishment or rewards, preferring simply to spend as much quality time with your child as possible. It's understandable that you want to spend your energy doing positive, loving things with your children. Keep in mind, though, that consistent limits provide structure in a chaotic world and reinforce which behaviors are acceptable. Children of every age will benefit from your understanding of the emotional crisis your illness poses for them. Your understanding of their need for consistency and limits lets them know that the need for order in their world has not changed just because you are ill.

Infants from Birth to Two Years Old

What They Understand and How They React:
Infants care primarily about having their own needs met.

In the first few months of life, babies are focused on having their own needs for food, warmth, sleep, and nurturance met. They will become fussy if there is a significant change in the way you treat them or if you are less able to give them affection.

Newborns can be quite sensitive to changes in their environment, including emotional changes, so when your partner or you are under stress, your baby will probably experience some stress, too. He may cry more frequently and have periods when he seems inconsolable. You may see changes in his eating habits such as trouble nursing or taking a bottle. Sleeping habits may also change, with your baby having trouble settling down for a nap or waking up in the middle of the night screaming.

If your baby goes for a long period without getting the attention and nurturing he needs, he may begin acting withdrawn and may stop responding readily or even push you away when you try to get his attention. The good news is that babies typically respond quickly in a positive way if someone steps in to provide consistent, affectionate care.

How You Can Help:
Provide nurturance and consistency.

Meeting the needs of an infant can be exhausting under the best of circumstances, and illness further compromises your ability and energy to do so. At this age your child can't understand anything you might tell him about your illness, so it is not what you say to your child but how you treat him that is most important. Even if your infant doesn't understand what you're saying on a cognitive level, though, he will pick up on the emotions communicated orally, so it's important to offer verbal assurances and support. It's also a good idea to refrain from discussing stressful topics with others in front of your baby.

While your baby won't know that you are sick, he will probably react to the loss in his life of a loving and playful caretaker. As much as possible, try to play with your baby, talk to him, and treat him as you did before you were ill. Do whatever it takes to energize yourself so that you can play with him and give him extra attention when you have the strength. But realize there will be some days when you may just be too tired or sick to play. When those days happen, make sure you arrange for your child to be with a stable, nurturing person.

Though you may have many offers from friends and family to care for your child when you are bedridden or hospitalized, try to leave him with the same person as much as possible. In addition, make any babysitters aware of the need to follow your child's previously established routine and to observe regular meal times and nap times. Prepare for a possible emergency by keeping a written schedule of your baby's typical day, and talk to the people who care for your baby about the need to be consistent and to express love and affection.

From Two to Four Years Old

What They Understand and How They React:
Toddlers and preschoolers can sense physical and emotional changes in you and may react with sadness or regression.

Developmentally, your child is beginning to explore the world and gain some independence from you. He is probably showing interest in other people, including other children. This desire to explore sets the stage for him to start going to school, where he will spend increasing amounts of time away from you, learning from and interacting with others. If he senses that his home base is not a secure place from which to explore the world, though, he may develop fears about being separated from you.

These fears, known as separation anxiety, are common to all children of this age, but they may be more intense if your child fears that your illness may make you unavailable when he needs you. He may cry or have temper tantrums when you attempt to leave him at daycare or with a sitter. He may want to sleep in bed with you, even if he previously slept in his own bed

71

every night. He may also do other things you thought he had outgrown, including sucking his thumb, having more frequent lapses in potty training, and clinging to you more than usual.

Your toddler or preschooler will probably be struck by your distress and physical changes and may try to comfort you when you are feeling bad. Toddlers are often attuned to obvious signs of illness or pain, and your child of this age may offer you Band-Aids, kisses, or whatever else he thinks might "fix" your illness. On occasion, he may get angry or blame you if he senses you aren't able to give him as much attention as you did before. He may tell you that you "aren't nice" anymore.

Your child might express specific fears about your illness, but look for him to do it in indirect ways. One four-year-old boy repeatedly played out a theme in which a woman doll had a "sick head." He did various things to cause her head to be "sick," including shooting it with a toy gun, then trying to fix it with bandages and operations. This boy's aunt had a brain tumor and, though he never mentioned his aunt or her illness directly, his play was an attempt to deal with it.

Very young children may seem confused and ask bizarre questions about your illness because of their limited ability to comprehend the medical and emotional implications. One three-year-old who caught the flu thought her own hair would fall out because she saw her mother's hair fall out during chemotherapy and was told, "It's falling out because Mommy is sick." Young children may ask the same questions over and over again, no matter how many times or how clearly you answer them.

Children in this age range also don't understand time the way adults do. If you tell a toddler that his father will be in the hospital for two weeks, you might hear him tell others that his father will be home tomorrow, or next year. He may be upset that his father does not return home soon, even though you have carefully explained how long the absence will be.

A toddler or preschooler might seem very sad if his parent's illness is prolonged and affects his life greatly. Their sadness may turn into anxiety and anxiety into frustration which can result in aggressive behavior such as biting or hitting. Attention spans are very short at this age, though, so don't be surprised if you see him crying or angry one minute and happily playing the next.

How You Can Help:
Use play, stories, and other creative means to explain the changes your child sees in you.

Children of this age rarely have the vocabulary to express their feelings or their understanding of serious matters. Watch your child play to see if he acts out themes of sickness, anger, sadness, or relationships between parents and children. Ask him to play with you, and use dolls, puppets, or stuffed animals to represent different members of your family coping with your illness.

Use dolls or draw pictures to help visualize your explanations. Hold up a doll and say: "This is Daddy. He has a bad sickness in his stomach. He goes to Dr. Patel to try to fix this sickness. Sometimes Daddy is very tired after he has been to see Dr. Patel, so he has to rest by himself for a while."

You can also use play to let your child know that, whatever happens, he will be cared for. You might pick up a doll and say: "What do you think would happen to Michael if his mommy had to go to the hospital for a while? How do you think he would feel about that? Do you think he might stay with Grandma and visit his mom a lot?"

Young children have some sense of right and wrong, but it is limited and rigid. Your child may think you became ill because you were bad and needed to be punished. When telling your child about your illness, assure him that you did not become ill because of something that you—or he—did wrong. You and others may have to tell him this repeatedly.

Comfort your child not only with words but also with hugs and kisses. Very young children understand physical comfort better than verbal comfort. Remind him often that you love him and that someone will always be there to take care of him.

As much as possible, help your child stick to his regular routine. Your illness may make you feel that you've lost control of your life. This feeling of lost control also affects your child, and major changes in his routine heighten this feeling. If he usually goes to his grandmother's after school, keep up that routine.

At the same time, you may need to establish new routines. If you are in the hospital for an extended stay, you could make Tuesdays and Saturdays the days he visits you. You can even set up a routine for the hospital visit itself. He could draw a picture for you before the visit, read a story with you during the visit, and get pizza with Dad on the way home. The routine will provide a structure within which variation can occur naturally, with a sense of security.

Toddlers and even some older children may react with regression or reversion to an earlier stage of development. Many parents get irritated or feel guilty if their child begins to act younger than his age, but regression is a normal reaction to stress. You may want to give in to regressive behavior for a short period (say, two to four weeks). Sometimes "babying" a child a little reminds him that he is safe. For example, if your four-year-old is having setbacks in potty training, it is okay to let him sleep in a pull-up for a little while.

Often young children want to sleep in their parents' bed during times of stress. There are varying opinions—many equally valid—about whether this is a good idea or not. Some people believe that sharing a bed can be a bonding experience and make your child feel safe during times of stress. Others, however, feel that children of this age should be encouraged to sleep alone to prevent over-dependency and further regression. It can be very hard to get children to go back to their own beds once they're used to sleeping in yours, so consider what's going to happen when you decide you really need to sleep alone.

If you are opposed to co-sleeping and your child resists sleeping in his own bed, try spending a little more time with him at bedtime, reading stories, singing, and cuddling. You can also put a blanket and pillow on your floor or outside your room in case he feels he can't make it through the night alone. Make it clear from the outset, though, that this is a temporary arrangement to help him through a difficult time.

If you believe that co-sleeping provides a sense of safety and security for you and your children, be sure to also make the most of the waking time you spend with your child. It is natural for parents to want to comfort children by co-sleeping, but be aware that you may be trying to meet your own emotional needs. That's okay as long as your child is comfortable with it. Keep in mind that when you and your child are both asleep, you are not really spending quality time together.

Watch to make sure your child's frustration, sadness, or anxiety isn't manifesting itself in aggressive behavior. If he is biting or hitting, let him know quickly that such behavior is not appropriate. Let your child's daycare provider or preschool teachers know what's going on with you. Ask them to let you know if they see any significant changes in your child's behavior or mood. If they do, make a plan with them to help your child deal with his feelings—whether by giving him a hug when he is looking sad, or redirecting his attention when he seems to be on the verge of losing his temper.

Answering Your Two-to-Four-Year-Old's Questions

Typical questions children of this age ask reflect their empathic understanding that something is wrong with you and their desire to comprehend more fully the nature of the problem. Their questions reveal their fears in the face of their inability to grasp the complexity of illness.

Some typical questions children this age may ask are:

What made you get sick?
Why are you sick?
Are you going to get better?
Does it hurt?

Questions about what made you get sick might be answered with a simplified medical explanation. For example, "I have a sickness in my belly, and I have to take medicine to make it go away. The medicine has to be strong to make me better, so for a little while it's also going to make me sick."

More difficult to answer are questions about *why* you are sick. Whatever you decide to tell your child, your answers should be simple, direct, and honest. For example, "I don't know why I got sick. I didn't do anything to cause this, but sometimes people just get sick for no good reason. I know it must be confusing to you. It is to me, too."

Be prepared to answer the same questions repeatedly, and be prepared for your child to misinterpret what you tell him. Encourage the rephrasing of these questions for greater clarity and to lessen the likelihood of misinterpretation. In any case, your patience is essential, and knowing in advance that it will be tried can be helpful.

Children in this age range may also ask blunt questions about changes in your appearance. Don't be surprised if your appearance seems to be their primary concern. Try to remember that this is developmentally appropriate and as much as possible don't take it personally.

You might want to talk to your doctor or hospital social worker about simple and effective ways to answer specific questions about your illness. Many hospitals also provide pamphlets written for children to explain various illnesses.

From Five to Eight Years Old

What They Understand and How They React:
Children of this age have a growing understanding of the causes and effects of illness. This limited understanding may cause some fear and confusion, but also don't be surprised if your child shows no obvious behavioral or emotional reaction.

At this age, children tend to react to a parent's illness primarily with sadness. They have strong opinions about what sort of behavior is acceptable for them. For instance, your child may try to conceal his sadness or fear in an effort to seem grown up and then disappear into his room to cry rather than share his feelings with you. Family members who notice such a change might say that he acts "spaced out" or that he has begun to isolate himself.

Often children of this age have trouble voicing or showing their distress and react by withdrawing from others. They may show physical signs of stress, including complaints of stomachaches and headaches. As a result, you might miscalculate how deeply your child is affected by your illness and thus fail to give him the support he needs.

Children of this age may also try to become self-reliant and more helpful when they are worried about you. This reaction can be positive because it's helpful to you and may allow him to regain a sense of control over his life. It can be a problem, though, if he tries to act like a parent himself in an attempt to shut out his need to be nurtured. Developmentally, children at this stage aren't ready to take care of themselves, and growing up too fast can pose problems for them later on.

At this age it is important for children to feel competent and smart. They usually try to be helpful and can show great empathy and support. They may get frustrated, though, by things they don't understand or can't do.

Your child of this age will have some limited understanding of your illness and its implications. Because of this, he may be more vulnerable than younger children because he is still not mature enough to cope with what he knows. Children in this age range often fear that they will lose control and be forced to give up the independence they have only recently achieved. This fear often results in denial; in other words, he may pretend that he doesn't know anything is wrong with you. Denial may also result in other fears that, on the surface, seem unrelated to your illness, such as fear of the dark or of going to sleep. Some children develop a fear of going to the bathroom or bathing alone.

Confusion is a common reaction for children in this age group. Because he doesn't have a clear understanding of the reason for your illness (some simple cause-and-effect relationship such as getting burned by touching a hot stove), he may ask questions such as,

Why did you get sick?
Am I going to get sick, too?
Is Mom going to get sick, too?

Blaming someone or something for your illness is one way your child may attempt to explain why you got ill. He may think he caused your illness because of something he did to you or angry thoughts he had, and he may need to be told frequently that this is not the case. He may feel guilty for his imagined sense of responsibility. It might help him to know that other children's parents become sick and that all families experience difficulties from time to time. This will also help with the anxiety that your illness will make him seem different from his peers.

Worrying about the vulnerability of other family members, especially his other parent, may make your child regress and become clingy. A six-year-old may talk baby-talk or want to be held more.

How You Can Help:
Let your child know it's okay to feel sad or frightened when a parent is seriously ill.

Explain in simple, clear language that you are sick. Explain what type of sickness you have and what you are doing to try to get better. Let him know that many aspects of your illness are confusing or hard to understand, and you expect that he will have questions about it. If you have trouble understanding some things about your illness or treatment, it's okay to let him know that.

Talk about how your illness may affect your child and what you are going to do to make sure his needs are met. Explain any possible changes in his daily routine. For example, tell him who will take him to school in the mornings, who will make his lunch, and who will take him to karate if you are too sick to do these things.

If your child acts overly self-reliant, or if he acts like a parent to younger siblings, thank him for his help but also gently remind him that he is still a little boy himself. If your illness has caused him to have increased responsibilities at home, let him know that you appreciate how helpful he is but that his main responsibilities are to work hard at school and to play with his friends and siblings. Let him know that you do not want any of these things to change as a result of your illness.

You may also need to give your five-to-eight-year-old permission to express his grief over the way your family has changed. If you notice changes in your child's behavior, make a point of telling him clearly and repeatedly that it is normal to feel bad when a parent is sick. Help him express his feelings in creative ways, such as drawing, performing a puppet show, or playing out scenarios with dolls.

If your child starts acting a lot younger than his age, be patient. For a few weeks respond positively to his regression by comforting him physically, holding him, or rocking him to sleep. At the same time, though, try to talk to him about what is causing him to feel insecure. You might say, "Sometimes when children are worried that their parents won't be able to take care of them, they act much younger than they really are. Do you think that might be why you are afraid right now?" You may also need to reassure him that his other parent will probably not become ill any time soon.

If your child starts acting like he is afraid to leave your side, let him know that you understand that he worries about you when he is gone, but that he needs to go to school and do his other activities. Remind him of things he likes at school, such as playing with friends. Ask questions about his friends, games, or school projects to encourage his interest in something other than you. Let him know that it's okay to still play and have fun and enjoy other areas of his life. Giving in to his fear and allowing him to stay home will only validate his fear. Although it might appease him temporarily, it could make him more afraid and anxious in the long run. When he does go to school, if he is taking his strong emotions out on his peers by fighting or yelling at them, let him know that you understand his frustration but that he needs to play nicely. Let his teachers know what is going on with you, and ask them to report any changes in his behavior or mood to you.

Answering Your Five-to-Eight-Year-Old's Questions

Children in this age group may ask specific questions about the medical aspects of your illness. Explain that a lot of the details are confusing, but he can ask you about anything he doesn't understand. Let him know that there are some aspects of your illness and treatment that you don't understand yourself.

Your child might ask,

Why is your hair falling out?

Did I do something to cause you to get sick?
How did you get cancer?

Be specific and clear in your answers:

I have a disease called multiple sclerosis. The doctors don't really know what causes multiple sclerosis, but it's a disease where my own body sort of fights itself. What happens is that a certain area of my brain and spinal cord gets sick, and that makes my brain not work quite right. I get tired and weak, and sometimes I might not be able to stand upright or balance myself. It might affect my eyesight and maybe other things, too. Everyone with MS has different symptoms. MS isn't something you can catch, and it isn't going to kill me. Most people with MS are able to work and live for fifty years after they are diagnosed.

If a child of this age asks you if he caused you to get sick, just simply state: "No. Nothing you did could possibly have caused me to get sick."

From Nine to Twelve Years Old

What They Understand and How They React:
Fear of seeming dependent and helpless may make your child act irritable and bossy or more grown up than he really is.

Many parents view this stage as the calm before the storm of adolescence. Typically, children of this age might be occasionally moody, headstrong, and uncommunicative, but they are primarily moving toward more independent decision-making. Your preteen may have discovered, for example, that you can't make him do his homework if he has told you he doesn't have any.

Puberty typically begins during this developmental stage, and with that comes a host of issues and challenges. With the many physical and emotional changes inherent to puberty comes an increased self-consciousness. Preteens often feel that everyone is watching them. Your preteen may feel resentful of you if he believes your illness sets him apart from his peers or makes him seem different from them.

A preteen may react strongly with expressions of shock, anxiety, sadness, anger, or disgust to big changes in your appearance or energy level. For example, your eleven-year-old may tell you your skin is ugly if it is affected by chemotherapy.

If your preteen fears you can no longer take care of him, he may start acting very responsible and try to take over parenting roles. He may become controlling and bossy. These attempts to deal with feelings of helplessness may alternate with feelings of guilt about how he is treating you and with expressions of sadness and concern for you.

Your child may seem more withdrawn as he copes with your illness. Some children work hard to hold their emotions in and hide them from their parents and others. Many parents report that their children of this age become more quiet than usual or spend more time alone than they previously did. This can be their way of coping with stress and should be monitored.

When faced with a parent's illness, children of this age may worry about their own health and imagine that minor problems are very serious. They may also develop phobias not related to illness at all. They may have trouble falling asleep or wake up with nightmares. They may have trouble concentrating in school, keeping up with homework, or performing on tests as well as they used to.

Children of this age begin to have a natural developmental movement toward increased independence from family as peer relationships become increasingly more important to them. However, they still need to feel their parents are there for emotional refueling. This process can be threatened when a parent is ill. Your illness and the changes it brings to your child's life may awaken feelings of childishness and helplessness in him. He may believe that these feelings must be controlled because he wants to appear independent and strong. The frustration these conflicting feelings arouse may cause him to act angry or irritable about things that seem totally unrelated to your illness. You and other people in his life might not realize that this behavior is an expression of his grief over your illness, and this may prevent him from getting the understanding and empathy he needs. Sometimes your child may just want to cuddle and talk to you, but you may have to be the one to make the first move.

How You Can Help:
Recognize your child's need to mourn the changes in his life and encourage him to communicate his feelings.

Spending a little extra time talking to your preteen will go a long way toward helping him cope better with your illness. Make the first move toward open communication because you can't expect a child of this age to seek you out when he is feeling bad. Let him know that you understand how hard your illness is for him and encourage him to express how he feels, even if his feelings are negative. A preteen needs to mourn the changes that have taken place in his family and to have others show him they understand what he is going through. He needs to share his longing for things to return to normal and to have those feelings validated. Often, feelings of loss go unrecognized by others, particularly if your child works to conceal them. Actively encourage him to talk or draw pictures expressing his feelings, and let him know that negative feelings about your illness are normal and acceptable.

Let your preteen know that you sometimes feel sad, angry, and frightened, too. Let him know that you miss doing the things you used to do with him. Remind him of any positive aspects of the situation. For example, you might say, "It makes me sad, too, that I haven't been able to watch you play basketball in the park much this year. I have loved seeing how much Grandpa looks forward to taking you, though. It has really given him a chance to get to know you in a different way, and that makes me happy."

When you feel well enough, make sure to spend some one-on-one time with your child. A lunch for just the two of you or a trip to get ice cream can go a long way even if he appears sulky or withdrawn. If you have more than one child, be sure to create alone time with each of them.

If your preteen seems resentful because your illness makes him different from his peers, try not to take it personally. This reaction is a normal part of his development, more a result of his own self-consciousness than of anything you have done wrong. While you should acknowledge his feelings, you should not tolerate rudeness. If his frustration causes him to treat you or others inconsiderately, discipline him as you would if you were not ill. For example, you might say, "I know you're frustrated that I can't help the other mothers with the class party. But that is no excuse for being rude to me. I won't tolerate that kind of language."

If your preteen acts unaffected by your illness, it's not because he isn't aware that you are sick or because he doesn't care; it's more probable that he can't begin the process of mourning the changes in your family until he feels stable and secure again. Such stability might come from establishing a relationship with an adult (aunt, teacher, counselor, parent of a friend, etc.) who can make him feel secure enough to express his sadness over these changes. Encourage relationships with responsible, loving adults who can help this process along.

Answering Your Nine-to-Twelve-Year-Old's Questions

Your preteen may ask very few questions about your illness, but that doesn't mean he doesn't have any. He is probably pondering how your illness will affect his life, and yours. Even if your child doesn't bring up these questions, we suggest you answer them anyway. Typically, he may worry about several issues, and may ask questions such as:

> *Can I catch what you have?*
> *How is your sickness going to affect my life?*
> *Are you going to die?*
> *Will I get to see you when you're in the hospital?*
> *Do I have to go to the hospital?*
> *Who's going to take care of me if something happens to you?*

Whenever possible, try to answer the unspoken but implied question that lies behind what is voiced. For example, if he asks if you will die, you might say:

I am not expecting to die, and I am going to do everything in my power to make sure that doesn't happen. But I understand why you are worried about that. I know I have to be realistic because with this disease there are no guarantees. What I can promise is that if something changes, I will tell you.

Adolescents from Thirteen to Eighteen Years Old

What They Understand and How They React:
Denial, pretended indifference, embarrassment or anger are typical reactions teens have to a parent's serious illness.

The major developmental task of adolescence is to form and refine a cohesive sense of self. Teens typically achieve this task by trying out different roles and then discarding them or integrating them into their personalities. As they become more independent from their parents, it can be a rocky time, particularly when parents don't recognize the need for more autonomy or when the teen makes irresponsible decisions.

There are a lot of different ways a teenager might react upon learning about a parent's serious illness. They might be embarrassed by their emotions and attempt to hide them, either by acting like they don't care or by acting stoic and overly mature. Conversely, your teen might be frightened by the news and cry dramatically. In either case, he may well need more physical affection and support than he has previously wanted or needed.

Anger may not be the initial reaction, but it is possible that your teen might get mad and slam things around or storm out of the house. It is often easier for a teenager to express anger or indifference than sadness or helplessness.

Anger or pretended indifference can give your teen a fragile sense of power to counteract his feelings of helplessness. If these strong emotions lead to aggressive acts, though, your child may begin to have problems with peers, teachers, or other family members. Acting indifferent or angry can also cause your teen to become depressed, particularly if he never acknowledges his underlying sadness and fear.

Your child may also react by trying to avoid difficult or emotionally intense situations because his feelings overwhelm him. This avoidance may make him seem indifferent and uncaring. Sarah, a sixteen-year-old whose father became sick and lost his hair suddenly, seemed cold and removed about the illness. Her father was frustrated, saying, "She has shut off her emotions entirely. I don't know how to get her back." Eventually, after much discussion, he realized that she actually cared very deeply, and her distance and coldness were defenses against the intensity of her emotions.

Your teen may pretend that nothing unusual is going on. Such denial can help him take care of himself and continue to succeed socially and academically, but it could cause problems if your illness gets worse. He may have a rude awakening if he has not already been thinking about how your illness affects his emotions and his life. Denial could prevent him from dealing with powerful emotions that may cause problems later in life. One teen said:

> *Even though it was only a few years ago, I can't remember a thing about the two years my father was ill. I was in a complete fog, even though I know I seemed pretty normal on the outside. I was in denial then, and I still am. I know that my fear that he was going to die has somehow affected*

my ability to trust people, but I just don't talk about it or think about.

It is possible to suppress really strong emotions for a long time, but we can't do it forever.

Denial may take the form of putting a lot of energy into activities that keep teens from admitting that something is wrong. They may get involved in more school activities, sports, and clubs, and this can be a healthy coping skill. Keep an eye on your teen to make sure any new activities are not harmful ones, like drinking or drug use, or even less harmful ones such as neglecting to do homework.

You may feel like your teen is shutting you out. He may be unwilling to discuss your illness with you, in part because he does not want to upset you or make things worse for you. When they are feeling frightened or sad, teens typically turn to their friends for support, which can be a positive way of coping. Their friends, however, won't fully understand what they are going through, unless they have lived through the same experience themselves. If your child seems to respond best to advice from people his own age, consider finding a support group for him so he can get feedback from his peers under the guidance of a trained professional.

The feelings your illness arouses in your adolescent may clash with the tasks of this stage of development. Adolescents of seriously ill parents often feel guilty about normal rebelliousness and withdrawal from the family, even when such behavior had been occurring prior to the illness. Guilt may cause teens to act rebellious one minute and to make exaggerated attempts to act like concerned, mature adults the next.

Your teen may also begin having headaches and other psychosomatic illnesses. He may do things designed to punish himself, to get others to take care of him, or to release tension, such as sexual promiscuity, drug or alcohol abuse, or self-mutilation.

Your adolescent may also feel guilty for doing perfectly acceptable things, like going out with friends. Michael, a seventeen-year-old whose father had cancer, told us: "I went to the beach with my friends for the weekend, and even though it was fun, I felt terrible after. I felt like I should have spent that time visiting my dad in the hospital, or maybe helping my mom."

You might want to explain that while you want to spend meaningful, intimate time with your teen, you also expect him to do normal teenage things, such as extracurricular activities and hanging out with friends. Be clear about your expectations: "I know that you love me and want to take care of me, but it is important for you to have a social life. I would like you to have dinner most nights with the family, and that's when we will visit and catch up."

The natural turmoil involved in adolescent development combined with the emotional upheaval created by your illness may cause your teen to feel besieged. One sixteen-year-old girl said:

> I felt so overwhelmed I didn't know what to do with myself. I remember my father calling me at school to tell me my mother had cancer. No one else knew, and I left school and drove myself to the hospital. On the way, I stopped at McDonald's and bought all this junk food. I just sat in the hospital parking lot, cramming food in my mouth, not knowing what else I could do to make myself feel better.

Your teenager is in the process of figuring out who he is, apart from you and the rest of the family. He is developing a personal style of dealing with problems, based in part on what he has learned from you, in part on peer influence, and in part on the culture to which he has been exposed (books, songs, television, movies, etc.). Your illness may challenge his ability to develop new personal values and newfound independence. While he is able to understand the causes and effects of serious illness as adults do, he may not have the confidence or experience to know how to respond to such a crisis.

How You Can Help:
Let your teenager know that whatever his reactions to your illness, you realize it is hard on him and you are available to talk if he needs you. Also, let him know that you appreciate the support he gives you.

Let your teenager know that his support means a lot to you, and accept his offers of help. He may be able to express support best by running errands for you or by taking you to the doctor, rather than through verbal or emotional displays.

Tell your child that you understand that your illness affects his life, and encourage him to talk about his feelings. At the same time, recognize his need to separate from you and the rest of the family on occasion. Encourage him to spend time with friends and to have fun and socialize.

Don't excuse rebellious or rude behavior just because it may, in part, be a reaction to your illness. Use the same discipline you would if you were not ill, but temper it with an understanding of how your illness has affected your teen's life. You may say:

I know things have changed a lot since I got sick, and that is hard for you. That is no excuse for your staying out all night, though. Any feelings you have are acceptable, but that sort of behavior is not. There are consequences to what you did last night. What can I do to help you find more constructive ways to express your feelings?

If your teen seems to be struggling emotionally, suggest healthy outlets. Volunteer work has been proven to increase self-esteem and overall wellbeing, and your child's school counselor should be able to direct him to community service opportunities. Doing art and journaling are healthy activities that many teens use to express difficult emotions. There is strong evidence that exercise has positive effects on mental health; encourage your child to play school sports, go for regular walks or runs, or find any other physical outlet he enjoys. You may also want to talk to your teen to see if he would be interested in a program devoted to outdoor education, such as Outward Bound. Although these programs can be costly, they often offer substantial scholarships. Claire, a young adult whose mother had serious health complications throughout much of Claire's childhood, told us,

I was depressed and completely lacking in self esteem as an adolescent. All the years of my mother's illness were really taking a toll on me. My aunt finally suggested Outward Bound, and I think that might have saved my life. I gained confidence in my own ability to take care of myself, made new friends, and returned home a totally different person. I still use what I learned from that experience as an adult.

While some teens will want to be home with you when you are sick, others may need a break from dealing with the intensity of the situation.

Above all, be honest with your teenager about your illness. Provide details about the causes and effects of the illness, your prognosis, and your course of treatment. Let him know about any changes in your condition. Involve him as much as possible in decisions to be made for the family, and show him you respect his opinions. Let him know what you are doing to fight your illness and to take care of yourself, both physically and emotionally. He may not show it, but he is interested in how you are dealing with your illness, and by watching you he will learn how to take care of himself, even when situations are out of his control.

Tell your teen that you are there for him if he needs to talk, get a hug, or get any other kind of emotional support. Let him know, however, that you recognize that he may need it less than he did when he was younger. If he backs off and seems uninterested in your illness, recognize that this is a typical way that teenagers cope, but continue to update him as your health changes or when you begin new treatments.

Ask your adolescent if he would like to speak with a counselor or a religious leader trained to help people deal with problems. Check into what kinds of adolescent group therapy are available in your community. It may help your child to meet other teens who have experienced similar problems. Consider whether your child would feel more comfortable talking with a family friend rather than a professional. If this is the case, help him identify a suitable adult with whom to share his feelings. Talk to your child about the various resources available to help him deal constructively with the emotional effect your illness has on him.

Answering Your Adolescent's Questions

Your teen may have many questions that weigh heavily on his mind, but he may be reluctant to voice them. Whether he asks directly or not depends on his personality and on your ability to communicate with him. Some things he might be wondering are:

> *How are you feeling?*
> *How is this illness going to change you?*
> *How will your illness affect my daily life?*
> *What treatments and medications are you having, and do they work?*
> *Can I tell my friends about this?*

It may be a good idea for you to answer the questions you think your teenager might have, regardless of whether he asks them or not. For example, you may say, "I want to talk to you about my illness. I have been thinking about some of the questions I might have if I were in your situation."

Your answer should include as much information as you feel comfortable giving. You might tell your adolescent daughter,

> *You probably know that the cause of breast cancer can be genetic, and you might be wondering if you have a higher chance of getting it since I have it. The chances you will get it just because I did are slim, but you are at an increased risk. There are tests that can tell you if you carry the gene for the disease, but even if you do carry the gene, it doesn't mean you will definitely get breast cancer. Some people get breast cancer without having the gene, and some people have the gene but never get the disease.*

This is difficult stuff because of the uncertainty, but it is better for a teenager to have an enlightened uncertainty than to worry alone in total darkness.

Whatever your child's age, the most crucial element affecting his ability to cope with your illness is communication. Pay attention to words and behavior. Listen and look for signs of struggle. Through both verbal and nonverbal means, share your own thoughts and feelings, inquire about his thoughts and feelings, and be as open, honest, and loving as possible.

Dos and Don'ts for **Getting Children Through It**

- *Do* tell your child that you are ill, and if he is old enough to understand, give him details about what your treatment will be.

- *Do* keep in mind that children have a wide range of "normal" reactions to a parent's illness.

- *Do* answer your child's questions honestly, using simple, straightforward language.

- *Don't* be surprised if you have to answer the same questions repeatedly, especially with younger children.

- *Do* make time to play with your child as much as possible.

- *Do* continue to ask your child how he is feeling, even if he says he is just fine.

- *Do* indulge your young child somewhat if he begins acting younger than his age.

- *Do* give your child extra attention and affection.

- *Do* be consistent with your rules and expectations, but also understand that new routines may be necessary.

- *Don't* give your child more household responsibilities than a child his age can handle.

- *Do* remind your child that schoolwork must remain a priority.

- *Don't* let your children isolate themselves from their peers.

- *Do* provide your child with opportunities to connect with other adults and children.

- *Do* continue to discipline your child when necessary, while acknowledging that he is going through a difficult time.

- *Do* recognize your teen's increasing need for independence, and discuss how your illness might be affecting that need.

- *Don't* turn a blind eye to high-risk behaviors such as drinking, drugs, skipping school, or self-injury.

Cancer – A Love Story

Leilani was diagnosed with lobular breast cancer in the summer of 2014. After a false negative mammogram, a false negative MRI, and multiple fights with her insurance provider, she was exhausted even before she had the surgery that involved a double mastectomy and the discovery of cancer in sixty-four lymph nodes. Two weeks after that surgery, Leilani's husband, Ed, learned that he had colon cancer and needed surgery immediately. Leilani admits that she "lost it" at that point. She says, "I thought to myself, 'I can't bathe myself or feed myself. I can't even reach the cereal bowls in our cabinets. Who the hell is going to take care of me?' I expected to be treated like a queen for a couple of months while I recovered. I had no idea how we were going to handle this."

In addition to the implications of their illnesses, Leilani also worried about the logistics of caring for her eleven-year-old son, Max, whose school year had just started. Her two older sons were not available to help: Sam, eighteen, had just started college in another city, and Ben, twenty-two, was working in another country. She was going to need to rely heavily on extended family and friends, but when she began telling others about her family's crisis, they seemed overwhelmed. She states that, "A lot of people still think cancer is a death sentence. Some of our friends couldn't deal with it, and we ended up comforting them, instead of the other way around."

The stress was really taking a toll on both Leilani and Ed. Leilani reached out to a friend she thought would understand by sending a private message on Facebook. After communicating back and forth with Leilani, the friend told her, "I think this is your and Ed's love story. You've always done everything together, and you're going to get through this together, too." That statement rang true for Leilani. Looking at the situation in this way helped push her into "survivor mode" and helped her reframe both her approach to fighting cancer and the way she communicated her struggles to those around her.

Leilani turned to the Internet and social media to get ideas about how to deal with her diagnosis in a positive way. "I didn't want to just curl up in a fetal position and let it take over my life, and I certainly didn't want to model that sort of behavior for my children." Websites and Facebook pages devoted to handling illnesses proactively inspired her to find ways she and her family could reintroduce a bit of humor and fun into their lives. She used Facebook to post pictures and regular updates on Ed's and her treatments, and the supportive responses people made to these postings made her feel less isolated when she was bedridden for long periods. She posted a film that she and Max made in which she dressed up like a superhero and defeated the cancer monster. The entire family visited a hair salon and dyed pink and blue streaks in their hair. When her hair began falling out, Max shaved her head and posted photos on Facebook. These actions, whether silly or symbolic, helped Leilani and her family gain a sense of control over what was going on in their lives. "I started viewing our illnesses and our treatments as a journey our family was on together, and I was going to do my best to make sure we had a little fun on that journey."

The Internet also provided a convenient way for Leilani to coordinate the logistics of her family's lives. Their church used Sign-up Genius to coordinate meals and transportation with the family. The parents of Max's school friends drove him to and from school, and Leilani was able to email or text them when there were necessary schedule changes.

Leilani notes that she and Ed had to stay away from reading too much about their illnesses on the Internet, though, because that did nothing but scare them. Still, she can't imagine what her experience would have been like if she hadn't had the Internet to facilitate her efforts to cope both emotionally and logistically with her family's crisis.

6. Information Technologies: A Mixed Bag

M any people turn to the Internet to research their diagnoses, and to a variety of information technologies to communicate with others about their illness and treatment. There are advantages to having such quick and convenient ways of transmitting and receiving information, but there can also be unintended negative consequences. It is a mixed bag, and this chapter explores how to sort out the benefits from the potential problems.

Researching Your Illness

No matter your diagnosis, an abundance of information is available at your fingertips. Just because you can use the Internet to read all about your medical situation, though, doesn't mean that you should. As one woman with breast cancer pointed out,

> *When I went to see the doctor the first time, he said, "you've probably done some research" and I said, "I've intentionally avoided that." I avoided it because I knew if I got online and started to research breast cancer I would see worst-case scenarios, and I really didn't know what to look for because I know there are different kinds of cancer, and I didn't want to put myself in panic mode.*

Spending too much time researching the possible implications of your illness could certainly increase your stress or worsen your physical symptoms. But some people don't even realize they need to go to the doctor until they start researching symptoms online. Doing some preliminary research helps them formulate questions to ask their physician and helps them understand treatment options.

Children are often more tech-savvy than their parents, so don't be surprised if your children research your illness online. Sometimes children are afraid to tell their parents that they have questions about the illness so they turn to the Internet for answers. It's a good idea to let your child know that there is a lot of medical information online but that much of it is inaccurate or may not apply to you. Encourage your children to be open with you if they have questions. You may want to suggest that they make a list and talk to your doctor about their concerns. If they do want to research your illness online, consider doing this with them so that you can direct them to the most accurate and useful sites.

Says one mother who had breast cancer,

My oldest child had mixed feelings about wanting to know details but being afraid of what she might learn, so, even though she had a lot of questions, she didn't ask me. But she researched the information online herself. I encourage my kids to research things. We do talk about the dangers of misinformation online, but I think they already kind of know that.

The unfortunate reality, though, is that there is a lot of confusing or inaccurate information online. It is important to consult trusted sites for reliable information. Some popular reliable websites for medical research are:

- *www.webmd.com*

- *www.healthcentral.com*

- *www.medicineonline.com*

- *www.emedicine.com*

- *www.health.discovery.com*

- *www.mayoclinic.org*

Sharing Through Information Technologies

Information technology has changed the way individuals and families share knowledge and get help when facing a serious illness. In the past, family members would write letters or telephone to update friends and family about treatments and progress. This could take hours or days and be physically and emotionally exhausting. Today, with email, group texting, and social media sites, we can disseminate messages instantaneously to large groups.

Liza, a mother of four, diagnosed with breast cancer, communicated with faraway friends.

I texted a small group of friends and said, "I had a bad mammogram. I'm having surgery, and I'm having a partial mastectomy. I wanted you all to know because lots of positive thoughts are good." And they all texted back, things like, "sending good thoughts," "so glad you told us," and stuff like that. They would shoot me periodic text messages asking how things were going, and that was nice. I also did a lot of text messaging with family. My cancer was so personal to them, and they had such strong feelings about it that text messaging helped me keep some distance. My sister would have preferred phone calls, but, the truth was, she gave me so much stress that using texts gave me some space, and that really helped me.

Email and texting spare us having to make telephone calls when we feel emotionally drained or do not feel like getting into a long conversation. Forwarding and cutting-and-pasting allow us to tell the story over and over, easily tailoring the main content of the message to individual recipients. Emailing allows us to copy to several recipients at once, and texting groups can cut down on needless repetition.

A potential downside is that texting and emailing can result in miscommunication. Rebecca, a mother of three, who had cancer, recounts what happened when she allowed a close friend to take charge of emailing regular reports to a group of concerned friends.

> *My friend started an email chain. She asked permission to do it, and I said yes, but I sort of assumed she'd put me on it, and she didn't. She got a little melodramatic with the emails, and it was scary for some people who started to ask me what was going on. I knew her heart was in the right place, but I asked her to begin to copy me on the emails. She was offended at first, like I didn't trust what she was writing. But, it's a tricky thing to write, in every way.*

If you decide to use information technologies such as email or texting to communicate with others during your illness, think carefully about who should be on group lists and how you can control what is shared. If you delegate the task, reserve the right to read and edit what is written and to set limits to protect your privacy.

Social media sites like Facebook allow families to communicate with a large audience while also maintaining some privacy and boundaries. If you are doing the posting, you can control what is being posted. Some family members or well-meaning friends may want to post their own updates on your status to gather support or to solicit prayers. Usually people have the best intentions, but you have the right to protect your privacy. Talk to your friends and family, and let them know your wishes. Be specific about what you want them to share or not share.

If your children have access to what you or others are posting about your illness, make sure you discuss these postings with them to clear up any concerns or confusion. Also, remind your friends and family that your children may see what they are posting. One mother with cancer reported using Facebook to reveal her diagnosis after initially keeping it within her family. It was a quick and easy way to get the word out, which she felt compelled to do after realizing her children were struggling, and their friends and their friends' parents didn't understand what was going on. This worked for her, and she was glad she did it: "I enjoyed hearing everyone say they were thinking of me and all that nice stuff. I didn't feel the need to reply and say thank you; it was more just something that was happening. It was easy to do a quick update to let them know how I was doing."

Using social media may not always have such a positive outcome. Marisol, a young mother with breast cancer, said,

I didn't use social media to communicate with others or share my journey. I didn't want people to feel sorry for me or think I was dying. In the middle of everything, I participated in an Avon Breast Cancer Walk. I was going through chemo at the time, but I left early because I couldn't stand being around people with cancer or relatives of people who had died from cancer. I only did it to support a friend who reached out and said she wanted to honor my journey. She

*used social media to do a lot of fundraising, and she talked
a lot about my illness on Facebook and Twitter. I thought it
would be rude to shut her down, since she was doing it for
a good cause. It was embarrassing. I didn't want people to
know my private business. I actually thought it was really
obnoxious; I felt used, and then I felt I had to support her by
doing the walk. I should have just stood up to her and told
her not to use me to make herself feel better.*

If ever there is a time when it is acceptable to put your
own needs first, this is it. Even if you consent to share personal
information, you have the right to shut it down at any point if
you become uncomfortable.

Using Information Technology to Organize Support

The past decade has seen the development of many online
opportunities to organize care for sick friends and family
members. This can include organizing food delivery, childcare,
home care, and drivers for doctor visits and treatments. Care
calendars that help coordinate support can take the burden off
family members and friends and also provide some distance for
parents who find it hard to accept help.

Some sites that are particularly helpful for organizing care
are:

- *www.caringbridge.org* helps create a website to send
  updates about the status of your illness and to arrange
  for support for your family.

- *www.takethemameal.com* provides online management
  for meal delivery.

- *www.signupgenius.com* allows people to build custom sign-up lists and sends email reminders.

- *www.carecalendar.org* helps you create electronic calendars that allow you to list and organize the help you need.

Lana is a teacher and mother of three whose school used *www.carecalendar.org* to coordinate meal delivery during her treatment for breast cancer.

> *One of the nice things was the kids at school would send notes with the food. They were involved. It gave them a way to be in contact with me, which was really cool. My own kids liked it because it was like Christmas every day. My kids are eaters, and they loved finding out what was for dinner each day. It wasn't leftovers every day. They were fed, and I didn't have to worry about it. The boys had hot food every night. We didn't have to ask them to go get fast food.*

Mass emails or group texts are another way that friends and family can take action by creating informal "helping networks." Often, friends and family members feel helpless as they watch you battle an illness. If you are reluctant to accept help from others, remember that letting loved ones—or even acquaintances and neighbors—help you makes them feel useful and involved in doing their part to fight your disease. Information technology can help.

Your Child's Use of Internet Social Media

Most children, especially teens, are frequent users of social media sites. This can be a good thing; it can provide a broad source of support which may keep them from feeling isolated as they struggle to deal with the emotions brought on by a parent's illness. Information technology can also provide a good way for you to stay connected with your child if you are receiving medical treatment away from home or if your children can't visit you in the hospital. Sofia, who sent her young children out of state to stay with her parents during a long hospitalization, kept in touch through FaceTime. "It was so hard for me to be away from my babies, but knowing my kids were safe and well cared for meant everything for me. It helped me focus on my recovery. We talked every day using FaceTime, and it made a big difference to actually be able to see their faces and for them to be able to see mine."

Despite the many advantages of using information technology and social media to communicate, you should discuss the potential hazards with your children. If you have information you prefer to keep private, you can tell your child that, while you encourage her to get the support she needs, you need her to respect your right to privacy. Be clear about your wishes and establish boundaries about what she can share. What used to be true, of keeping the "family business" private and out of the social networks of gossip, is now true of keeping details off the Internet. You may develop some "family rules" about sharing. For example, you might want to ask your child to tell you before she posts anything about you. Remind your child that what she posts can easily be shared outside of her own circle of friends. Keep in mind, too, that any messages you share with your own friends can easily be forwarded and seen by your children.

Lana's story illustrates how the Internet can be used to cause unintentional harm.

When I lost my hair, I didn't want to wear a real wig and pretend to be normal. Losing your hair is not normal, and pretending would have made me more self-conscious and uncomfortable. I borrowed some crazy wigs from a friend who uses them for costumes, and it was great, because when I had purple hair, no one noticed that I didn't have eyebrows or eyelashes. One night, we were out to dinner and I was wearing my purple wig. When I got home, my son said, "Hey Mom, did you have sushi for dinner?" I said, "Yes, how did you know that?" He said, "Well, I got a text, a Snapchat, from a friend, and it said to check out this lady with the purple hair." He went on to say, "I looked at the picture, and I had to do a double take. I thought, yep, that's my mom." He texted the girl back and said, "That's my mom. She has cancer, and she's wearing a purple wig because her hair fell out." So the girl responded, arguing that it wasn't his mom and it wasn't a wig; it was real hair. Finally, he sent her a picture of me in a different wig, with orange hair, and he said, "Yeah, here she is with orange hair. Her hair fell out because she has cancer." The girl apologized to him for months.

The Internet has transformed the way communities and individuals deal with illness. It provides rapid communication with large groups of people. It provides a way for friends and family to give ongoing support and encouragement without being overly invasive. And it provides many convenient ways to organize meal deliveries, shopping, and childcare. There can also be disadvantages, however, to having your private information shared publicly. *Know that you have the right to set boundaries at any time; your comfort and privacy are what are most important right now.*

Do's and *Don'ts* for Using Information Technologies

- *Do* research possible treatment options online but use only trustworthy sites.

- *Don't* assume that everything you read online is true or applicable to your situation. Stop reading if it makes you feel overwhelmed or paranoid.

- *Do* caution your children about the risks of doing medical research online. Encourage them to discuss with you what they find if they are doing online research.

- *Do* consider posting updates about your illness on social media if it might help garner support from friends.

- *Do* realize that your children may be turning to social media to get support.

- *Do* talk to friends and family, and let them know your wishes for how your personal medical information can and should be shared.

- *Do* consider asking one person to be in charge of online medical updates.

- *Do* have a family conversation to set guidelines about social media use as it relates to your illness.

- *Don't* feel like you have to agree if friends and family want to share your personal messages or health status online. You do not have to say yes to every request.

- *Do* ask someone to remove any post they make without your permission, especially if it makes you feel uncomfortable.

- *Don't* assume your child will not see posts or status reports about your condition.

- *Do* make use of online coordination sites to allow friends and family to provide support.

- *Do* consider that help can be organized online in many ways, including meal delivery, doctor visits, childcare, carpool, and group status updates.

- *Do* recognize that others want to help you and your family, and generally people do not offer what they don't want to give. Let them feel helpful.

7. When to Seek Counseling for Your Child

Many children are able to express and cope with emotions on their own and through discussions with their families. If your child is having trouble talking about his feelings about your illness, though, counseling is a good idea. Counseling should not, however, be used as a way to avoid family communication or to try to prevent your child from feeling anything unpleasant. Rather, it should be an option for children or teens who cannot or will not talk with their family, and it is strongly encouraged for those who are in danger of hurting themselves or others. Naturally, whether or not to seek counseling for your child is up to you and your partner, but you should also get your child's opinion about whether he thinks it might help him. Regardless of whether or not you have seen any changes in your child's behavior or mood, counseling could help if he thinks talking to a therapist might make him feel better. Therapy usually fails if children are completely unwilling to participate, but often they overcome an initial reluctance after one or two sessions, especially if you have found the right therapist.

To determine whether you should encourage your child to get counseling, ask yourself a few simple questions:

- How has your child's reaction to your illness affected other areas of his life such as school, friendships, and hobbies?

- Have his grades dropped significantly?

111

- Has he become withdrawn?

- Does he seem sad?

When considering your child's reaction to your illness, the line of separation between what is normal and what is excessive can be thin. The difference lies in the intensity and the duration of the reactions. If your child exhibits any of the following symptoms over several months, he may be in a major depression, and we suggest that he be evaluated by a mental health professional:

- Looks sad most of the time or cries much more often than before

- Seems tired or has trouble sleeping

- Worries a lot about his own health and has frequent minor complaints like headaches or stomach problems

- Has significant increase or decrease in weight

- Has significant changes in eating habits

- Seems not to care how he dresses or looks

- Isolates himself and avoids social activities

- Seems indifferent to school, friends, or hobbies he once enjoyed

- Says he feels life is worthless

- Begins abusing drugs or alcohol

- Acts angry or aggressive (yells, punches walls, fights with others)

You should immediately seek professional help for your child if he expresses suicidal thoughts or thoughts of hurting himself or others, or if you learn that he has been intentionally cutting or burning himself. These symptoms indicate that your child's safety may be at risk, and they should be taken seriously.

In our experience, many parents with serious illnesses believe their children would benefit from therapy but feel too sick or too distracted to actually get their children to weekly counseling sessions. If this is the case with you, it is certainly understandable, but consider whether you have some other options. Do you have a close friend or relative who could drive your child to his counseling sessions and be trusted to impart important information to you while respecting your child's right to confidentiality? Are there any agencies in your area that offer home visits by therapists? If you are in the hospital for an extended period or for frequent treatments, is there a therapist on staff who can talk to your child when he is there with you? Can your child's school counselor offer individual sessions?

If none of these options work for you, and if your child is not in any danger of hurting himself or others, consider seeking counseling *after* you have recovered from your illness to help him deal with some of the lasting effects your illness may have on him and on your family. A year after her treatment for breast cancer, Alex noticed that her five-year-old daughter, Emma, still seemed anxious about her mother's health. She decided to get counseling for Emma who revealed in play therapy that, during Alex's treatment, she felt that everyone else in the family knew what was going on, and she was the last to find out. "She told us, 'Sometimes I never find things out. Things happen and nobody tells me anything.' I was surprised to realize that she felt that way because she was so young, and I didn't think she really knew what was going on. I was glad she was able to express that in counseling."

Locating and Selecting a Mental Health Professional

If you decide your child would benefit from counseling, there are many ways to locate a therapist. Although the telephone book, the Internet, and your insurance provider's directory are full of listings, we recommend you get a direct referral from someone you trust. Your child's pediatrician, his school counselor, your own physician, and hospital nurses or social workers may all have good suggestions. Also, ask your clergy person or friends and family members about their successful counseling experiences.

There are many types of mental health professionals, and it can be confusing to tell the differences among them. Psychiatrists are medical doctors who can prescribe antidepressants or anti-anxiety medication, or locate physical or chemical causes for psychological problems. Psychologists, clinical social workers, marriage and family therapists and licensed professional counselors are all mental health professionals who provide counseling services and can make referrals to psychiatrists when necessary. Many of them can perform standardized tests to screen for depression and other problems. They should all have a master's degree (MA, MSW, MS, or MEd) or a doctorate (MD, DSW, or PhD) in the field.

Your child's therapist should either already have a license to do therapy or be working toward licensure under the supervision of a qualified, licensed mental health professional. Talk to the therapist beforehand to make sure she has experience working with children and teens. You may also want to ask whether she has experience working with grieving children and if she has ever worked with children whose parents are seriously ill. Before making a commitment to enter your child in treatment with a particular therapist, you will want to meet with that therapist to learn her qualifications and decide whether you and your child feel comfortable with her. This initial meeting is sometimes free of charge, but you should ask when you are scheduling it to make sure.

What to Expect from Your First Counseling Interview

Every therapist is different, but in the first session most will want to meet either with the parents alone or with the entire family. The private meeting with parents is likely if the children are very young. The first session typically lasts anywhere from forty-five to ninety minutes, and you will probably be charged a fee for it. In this session, the therapist usually conducts an assessment to collect information about your family as well as your child's medical and developmental history, school performance, social relationships, and family support.

Questions you should ask in the first session include:

- Can you tell me about your qualifications and experience?

- Do you have experience working with children my child's age?

- Do you have experience working with children who are grieving or whose parents are seriously ill?

- What do you expect of me? How often will we meet with you and when?

- How often will my child meet with you, and how long do the sessions last?

- What do we do in the event of an emergency? Can we contact you? How?

- If something is seriously wrong with my child, or if my child is in some sort of danger, will you tell me? What actions will you take?

- Will you speak with my child's school counselor?

- What is your policy about confidentiality? Do you share what my child says with me or with anyone else?

- What should I do if my child objects to coming to counseling?

- Do you specialize in a particular type of therapy or in particular problems?

After meeting with you and hearing your reasons for bringing your child to therapy, the therapist will usually tell you what type of treatment he recommends and how long he expects the course of treatment to be. Some common treatment therapies are outlined below.

Choosing a Type of Therapy

Really, what is most important is finding a qualified person you think your child will be able to relate to and trust. Study after study has shown that the relationship between the therapist and the client is the greatest predictor in determining the success of the treatment. That said, there is an array of therapeutic modalities to choose from, although the choice may not be yours to make. Typically, a therapist either specializes in a particular therapy or concentrates on a few types, adapting the treatment to what he thinks would best benefit each client.

The most common types of therapy being practiced today are group therapy, family therapy, and individual therapy. Each has its strengths.

Group Therapy

In group therapy, a small group of clients meets regularly, usually once a week, to discuss problems together and with the therapist, who serves as the group leader. Group members give each other suggestions and support and get insight into their own behavior and thoughts. Groups may be ongoing or limited to a certain number of sessions. Membership in the group may be closed once the sessions begin, or it may be open, allowing for new members to join along the way. If you are considering group therapy for your child or teen, look for a group with membership in the same age range as your child. It is also a good idea to find out what type of group it is and whether the members have problems similar to those of your child.

A typical reaction children or teens have when a parent is seriously ill is to feel that no one their own age could possibly understand what they are going through. This feeling can cause them to withdraw from their peers or act like nothing is the matter. If your child feels this way, group therapy may be a good choice for him. Groups are often especially beneficial for adolescents.

Family Therapy

Family therapy involves all members of a nuclear family, and possibly members of an extended family as well. There are many types of family therapy, but the most common is based on family systems theory, which emphasizes communication and relationship issues rather than the symptoms of individual family members. Family therapy may be particularly appropriate if your child is having behavior problems directly related to his feelings about your illness. It may be appropriate if the stress your family is under is causing you to blame each other, gang up on each other, or otherwise take out negative feelings on one another. Occasionally, a therapist may recommend that one or several family members participate in both family and individual treatment.

Your family may benefit from family therapy if you are experiencing a lot of overt conflict as a result of your illness. This treatment can also be helpful if your family has traditionally been reserved about discussing feelings, since these feelings now are naturally more intense and more difficult to handle alone.

Individual Therapy
Most individual therapies will involve your child meeting one-on-one and talking with a therapist once a week. If your child is a preteen or younger, the therapist will usually want you to play an active role in the sessions. You may come in together for part of each session, or the therapist may ask you and your child to come in at separate times. In therapy with adolescents you are often asked to take on a more distant role. The therapist concentrates on forming a private, trusting relationship with your teen, and often your teen will want to know that you are not trying to influence or prejudice the therapist in any way. You should not take this personally as rejection, since it is a normal part of the adolescent's development to crave privacy and attention to his individual needs. Individual therapy may be

more helpful than family therapy if you believe the problem lies not in poor family communication but in the sheer difficulty your child has coping with the negative feelings and major changes brought on by your illness.

Techniques and Theoretical Approaches Used by Therapists

Therapists draw on many different theories and techniques in their work. Which theory or technique is right for your situation will depend on many factors, so don't assume that one or another will be right for your child before talking with the therapist. Some common types of individual therapy are outlined below, but keep in mind that there are many other approaches from which to choose. You may want to ask your child's counselor what his approach is, and ask for clear explanations if there is anything you do not understand. You are entitled to know what you are getting your child into.

Play Therapy

Play therapy is the preferred treatment for children under the age of ten, who have not yet developed abstract reasoning skills and verbal abilities. Young children often understand things they cannot articulate. Since play comes naturally to children, your child can use play to show the therapist how he feels about himself and the important people and events in his life. In play therapy, the child usually sets the pace and decides the activities. The therapist is trained to interpret the themes underlying or motivating the play and to offer suggestions, both to your child and to you, to help resolve the problems that are revealed through the play. Play therapy does more than just reveal symptoms, though. By playing under the guidance of a therapist, children can often resolve their conflicts naturally and unconsciously through the process of creative expression.

Narrative Therapy

If your child's counselor draws on narrative therapy techniques, he will probably ask your child to tell stories about the problems he is facing. The narrative is then used to reveal symptoms and to plot the course of treatment. Narrative therapists contend that the telling of painful or problematic stories can help clients rewrite these stories to create new options for themselves. The idea is that, while you may not be able to control what happens in your life, you can control the way you deal with it and the meaning you ascribe to it.

Clients are encouraged to look at their problems as something separate from them, something that they need to tackle and revise, rather than something that is an essential or ingrained part of who they are. Creative techniques such as art and letter-writing are used to reframe the issues and create new perspectives and more hopeful attitudes. The therapist will actively collaborate with your child to solve problems in these ways. Because we use our creative and interpretive powers to deal with our emotions all our lives, narrative therapy is used with people of all ages.

Cognitive-Behavioral Therapy

Cognitive-behavioral therapy is based on the premise that irrational or faulty thinking is the cause of maladaptive behavior. If your child's therapist uses this approach, he will concentrate on hearing your child's thoughts and beliefs about your illness and helping him adapt those thoughts in order to change his emotional state.

Cognitive-behavioral therapists often assign homework to their clients. For example, a client may be asked to make a list of positive statements, usually called "affirmations," about himself. He may also be asked to actively concentrate on stopping negative thoughts and replacing them with more positive thoughts. For example, if he catches himself thinking negative thoughts about how your illness takes away from the time you spend with him, he may tell himself to stop thinking that way and instead concentrate on good times the two of you have had in the recent past.

This treatment can be extremely effective, but only if your child is willing to be an active participant in the process and to complete the homework assignments. Cognitive-behavioral therapy is used with all ages.

Psychodynamic Therapy
Psychodynamic therapy assumes that events that occur during a person's childhood shape personality development. This therapy is typically not as action-oriented as those mentioned above. Instead, through the context of the therapeutic relationship, your child's unconscious fears and desires will be brought to the surface. The therapist may offer some interpretation, with the idea that conflicts will resolve themselves once the client more clearly understands what emotions and events underlie any given behavior or feeling. Psychodynamic work with children and adolescents may involve the use of play, artwork, or dream recollection and interpretation to bring issues to the surface.

Paying for Therapy
Naturally, when selecting a therapist, you want to find the one who will work best with your child. However, cost is usually a

factor for most of us, and the fees therapists charge can vary widely. If you have health insurance, check to see whether it includes mental health coverage.

Questions you should ask your insurance company include:

- Do I have mental health coverage?

- Does the coverage include my children?

- What is my deductible?

- How many sessions will my insurance cover?

- What percentage of treatment is covered if I choose a provider outside the network?

- Does my insurance policy cover individual, family, and group therapy?

- How can I get a list of approved providers?

If you do not have mental health coverage, explore other options for you and your family. Many nonprofit agencies offer a sliding scale fee based on your income. Most counties have mental health clinics that may provide free or affordable counseling. Many public, government-run hospitals and university medical centers also have clinics, which may provide counseling for free or at reduced fees. Also, your child's school counselor may be able to provide some individual counseling at no charge.

The most expensive type of counseling will be with private practitioners, but cost varies greatly even among them. Some private practitioners offer reduced fees for a number of reasons, so it never hurts to ask if they offer them or if you qualify. Finally, if you feel a therapist's costs are too high, ask for a referral to another therapist who might consider your financial situation before setting a fee.

Dos and Don'ts for When to Seek Counseling

- *Do* ask your child if he thinks talking to a therapist would help him get through this difficult time.

- *Don't* use therapy as a way to avoid talking with your children about your illness or to protect your children from feeling anything negative.

- *Do* seek professional help immediately if your child expresses thoughts of killing himself or hurting himself or others.

- *Do* ask friends, family, or clergy if they can recommend a good therapist.

- *Do* talk to the therapist beforehand and, if possible, meet with her as well. You and your child should both feel comfortable with the person you select.

- *Do* make sure the therapist you select is qualified and experienced.

- *Do* remember that your child's relationship with the therapist is the most important factor in determining how successful the treatment will be.

- *Do* consider family therapy if your family seems to be having a lot of conflict.

- *Do* consider individual therapy for your child if he is having a hard time talking about his feelings and coping with your illness.

- ***Do*** check to see if your insurance policy covers mental health coverage. Find out specifically what that coverage includes.

- ***Don't*** assume that you can't afford therapy. Remember that school counselors and clergy often provide free counseling, and local agencies may offer therapy on a sliding fee scale. Private therapists sometimes reduce fees, as well; it doesn't hurt to ask.

Heredity and Disease

Understanding the Implications

When you are diagnosed with a serious illness, you may have questions about the genetic component to your disease and whether your children are at risk. You may want to discuss the possibility and desirability of genetic testing with your physicians. Sometimes, even if tests are available, it may not be a good idea to have them because, while there is a wide range of testing available today, there is not necessarily enough information about what can be done to help when someone tests positive for a particular gene. If your doctor agrees that genetic counseling is recommended for your family, there are genetic specialists in every state. You can find more information about how to find a genetic counselor in your area on the website for The National Society of Genetic Counselors, *www.nsgc.org*.

Chris Dvorak, MS, CGC, genetic counselor at the Hayward Genetics Center and Pediatrics Instructor at Tulane University, emphasizes that most cancers are not directly hereditary. They usually have multi-factorial causes related to the interaction of genetics and environment, but certain criteria do influence the likelihood of a hereditary component. These criteria include: strong family history of a disease, young age of onset, and unique presentation. There are tests that may be done to see if you are predisposed to certain cancers. The decision to have these tests is highly personal and should be done with great care and counseling from a trained professional.

If your disease is determined to have a hereditary component, you do not necessarily need to share this information with your child. Consider your child's age and maturity as well as whether or not she needs this knowledge at this point in her life. For example, while you may worry that your ten-year-old daughter could carry the BRCA gene that puts her at increased risk for developing breast cancer, there is nothing productive in terms of screening or prevention that she can do until she is older, and telling her may only cause distress. If your young child specifically asks about this issue, you might say, "This is something you don't need to think about at your age." On the other hand, if an adolescent asks, you may want to discuss the fact that there is a genetic/hereditary aspect to your disease and that there may be options she will want to pursue when she is an adult. Some genetic conditions do pose risks to children though, and in those cases it may be warranted to pursue testing at a younger age.

It can be stressful to know that you may have passed on a potentially disease-causing gene to your children. It may help to remember that testing positive for a certain genetic factor does not necessarily mean that they will develop the disease. You can do a great deal proactively to help ensure your children's continued good health, such as teaching them the benefits of exercise and good nutrition and making sure they have regular medical and dental checkups.

If you know that your children may someday benefit from having their genetic information available to them, we suggest that you keep detailed records of your medical reports, including any genetic testing you have had. You may want to create a special document with this information or include it in a living will that your children can access at the right age and time and under the right circumstances.

8. Coping with Terminal Illness and the Aftermath

While the focus of this book is on *living* with a serious illness, the sad reality is that sometimes a serious illness can result in death. In this chapter we discuss ways you can talk to your children about death because it is important to be honest with your children if your illness becomes terminal.

Many parents find it comforting to know they can take steps ahead of time to help their children understand and cope with their grief. Many also feel it is meaningful to plan ways to still have a presence in their child's future, particularly at significant milestones. This chapter offers some suggestions about how you and your partner can help your children deal with the adjustment to their impending loss. If you choose to skip the suggestions outlined in this chapter, don't worry: you're not a bad parent. If you think the ideas are good, but you lack the emotional or physical strength to carry them out, consider asking someone else to help you, such as your partner, another family member, or a close friend.

A Child's View of Death

While a child may have been naïvely unaware of all the comforts and supports that lent a sense of security to childhood, he or she is all too aware of the terrifying insecurity that marks life after the catastrophe of early death intrudes. If a loved and needed parent can disappear forever, then nothing is safe, predictable or secure anymore.

Beyond the immediacy of their personal loss, bereaved children must now make their way in a world itself marked by profound emptiness. The loss felt inside seeps out and engulfs everything.
—Maxine Harris, *The Loss That is Forever* (Plume, 1995, 6)

Though children almost always grieve when a parent is seriously ill, this grief naturally takes on a new shape and a new intensity if they realize that the illness will result in death. Most children, no matter how mature, have trouble accepting that their parents will die. Later in this chapter, we describe some specific reactions of children of different age groups. It is important to realize, though, that children of all ages typically respond with a combination of shock and disbelief, even if they have seen that you are very sick. One mother was in the hospital for over five months, but her teenage daughter never realized her mother might die until she went into a coma the week before her death.

Many children have never known anyone who has died, and their lack of experience can prevent them from grasping that their parent will be gone forever. Their intense need for the parent may cause them to pretend that death could not happen. They may act as if nothing is wrong or they did not hear the news. They may seem perfectly fine for a time, only to be overcome with emotion over something trivial or totally unrelated to your illness. One college student seemed fine, even a bit frantically cheerful, despite her mother's very poor prognosis. She continuously denied that she was having problems accepting her mother's illness, saying she knew the best thing was to continue going to classes, socializing, and working at her part-time job. When asked about her mother's illness, she reported the details matter-of-factly, and she seemed very distant. One day she broke down and began crying uncontrollably when she and a friend saw a dog almost get hit by a car. At that point her fear of losing control overcame her, and she began to move from denying her feelings to a great sadness.

Young children may not understand that death is permanent or what it really means, but they do understand when they have lost something valuable. As one six-year-old boy said, "My mommy says I can always talk to my daddy, so I do every night. I don't understand why he never talks back to me." Since they cannot understand an abstract concept like death, they may ask certain questions over and over, and some questions may seem bizarre. "Where will you live when you die? How does Mommy get food in the coffin? When will you come back?" Young children will focus on things relevant to their own lives. For example, one young boy circled his mother's casket before asking a funeral director, "Where does Mommy go to the bathroom?"

If your child sometimes seems carefree and happy even though you have told her you are dying, please know that this is a common coping defense for children. Even if they are old enough to understand death pretty clearly, they cannot sustain intense negative feelings for a long time. Think about how much shorter a child's attention span is than your own.

A recently widowed mother was dismayed when her children played with their friends at their father's funeral. She took their play as a sign that they did not truly understand that their father was dead, and she could not understand why they cried later that night and had trouble sleeping alone. Her eight-year-old son explained to her: "I couldn't take being so sad all the time. I needed to take a break and just play for a while."

Though your child is grieving, she is still a child and needs the release that play and laughter provide. It does not mean that she does not care, and if she seems sad or needy later, it does not mean that she is trying to manipulate you.

Your child might worry that she will forget you once you have died. You may want to tell her that with all loving relationships comes the gift of memory. While she may forget certain things about you as time goes by, she will never forget how much you love her or she loves you and all of the happy, loving times you have shared. She will also have pictures and keepsakes to remind her of you, and when she wants to feel close to you, she can hold those things and remember the special relationship that you shared.

"Who Will Take Care of Me?"

As much as your child loves you, a big part of her grief is going to be her concern about who will meet her needs, the needs you previously took care of. This is a concern for children of any age, though it will appear in different forms. A young child may worry about her other parent's health and whether that parent will also die. Reassure her by telling her that, while we will all die someday, her other parent is healthy right now, and there is no reason to believe that he will get sick or die soon. Assure her that her fears are normal but that her other parent is planning on being around for a long time to take care of her. David Techner, Director of the Kaufman Chapel in Detroit and a cancer survivor himself, suggests that it might comfort your children for the other parent to begin to have annual physicals and report the results to the children. Doing so not only shows that that parent is healthy, it teaches your child to take care of her own health by setting a positive example.

Children of all ages may worry about practical things such as whether they will have to move or who will take care of certain tasks you once managed. One young boy asked his father, "Who will do my laundry after Mom dies?" His father was able to tell him that he had arranged to have a housekeeper come in to do the laundry, and the boy was relieved that this task would be handled. Another father with cancer recalled his nine-year-old son worrying that his family would have to move if his father died because they would not be able to afford to stay in their home. His father explained that he had a substantial life insurance policy to protect the family in the event of his death. His son did not believe that such a thing was possible, so the father brought in the agent to explain how life insurance works. Once the boy realized he would be financially protected, he felt more secure.

When children express their needs, they often come across as frivolous or selfish. They can feel that their needs are selfish, too. Susan, a high school senior whose mother recently died of cancer, said that a thought that preoccupied her as she watched her mother die was: "Who is going to take me shopping for my prom dress?" Later, she had trouble shaking feelings of guilt and shame because of what she perceived as an inappropriate and shallow response to her mother's death. In fact, her thought was perfectly normal and perhaps unavoidable. Adults as well as children often revert to the trivial to avoid facing intense despair. In children and adolescents, this normal defense is coupled with an equally normal fear of what life will be like without their parents to watch over them. An important and fundamental fear can often be cloaked in a trivial-seeming disguise.

"I'm Going to Take Care of Everything."

Some children, on the other hand, seem to become selfless when dealing with a parent's illness and impending death. Assuming a pseudo-maturity, they start taking care of you and everyone else in the family. A five-year-old girl whose mother was dying told her older brothers: "Now I will be the mommy. I will cook for everyone, and clean for everyone, and take care of everything." She tried her best to do just that until her father finally convinced her that her most important job was to do well in school and to act like a little girl, not a mommy. Some parents unwittingly foster this in their children by saying things like, "Now you're going to be the man of the house." Statements like this can put a tremendous burden on children. It may make them feel better temporarily, but ultimately it places them in roles they are not developmentally ready to fill.

Perhaps the biggest danger children face when they are grieving the death of a parent is that they may learn to avoid love, fearing subconsciously that it will only result in loss. They may withdraw emotionally from others, so that they will not have to experience great pain. The problem with this reaction is that they will also not experience great joy if they do not allow themselves truly to connect with others. For this reason, you must help them address their grief. Whatever age your child is, she will probably respond to news that you may die by moving through the stages of grief. Keep in mind, though, that the way your child grieves will depend in part on her age, her level of maturity, and her previous experiences with loss.

We sketch below some reactions that may be seen in children of different ages. Remember that these are generalizations. Every child responds uniquely.

From Birth to Three Years Old

Infants and very young children have little, if any, ability to understand the permanence of death. They become distressed if no one cares for them in a consistent manner. They may seem sad or irritable when they feel abandoned. If a parent dies, they may cry whenever the surviving parent leaves the room, fearing that parent too will go away. Although they may not seem as disturbed as an older child, particularly if other adults are available to give them love, affection, and consistent care, they still grieve. Typical reactions include disturbed sleep patterns, changes in eating, increased irritability and tantrums, and frequent crying. Toddlers may become clingy and try to avoid going to preschool or staying with a babysitter. They may also repeatedly ask where the deceased parent is and when she is coming back, no matter how often things are explained to them.

From Three to Six Years Old

Children of this age also have trouble understanding that death is permanent, and they may repeatedly ask when they will see the deceased parent again. They may feel confused and may ask questions about why their parent died. They often have egocentric and magical thinking, which causes them to believe that something they did or thought caused the death. They may ask others if they caused the death or if they themselves will die. They may regress to previously outgrown behaviors such as bed-wetting, thumb-sucking, or baby-talking. They may become very clingy. It helps to talk to children of this age about death, to read them books that deal with or explain death, and to answer their questions, even if you have to answer the same questions over and over.

From Seven to Twelve Years Old

Children in this age range usually realize that death is final. They may be preoccupied by morbid thoughts about death and about what happens to the body afterwards. If the death was sudden or unexpected, it is not uncommon for children of this age to have brief hallucinations in which they see the deceased person or other figures, such as robbers or masked men. They may ask questions about what happens after death, or they may say nothing and act as though nothing has happened.

Children aged seven through twelve tend to take their cue by watching others around them, and their reactions will to some extent echo how others are responding to the death. They often want to seem more grown up about their response than they really are, and they may try to hide their true feelings. Often they pretend they are coping better than they are, and they may adopt a false air of maturity.

Children of this age may express their anxiety about death in indirect ways, such as through concerns about their own health and safety. If your child expresses concern that she will get sick and die, consider the following explanation:

When you get a cold or the flu, you are not going to die from that. Your body has special cells that fight the illness off. Most times when people get sick, they can either get better because their body can fight off the illness, or they take medicine that fights the illness. But sometimes, with a serious illness like I have, the body can't fight it. Just because I got this illness doesn't mean that you will get it.

Children in this age range may act out their emotions if they lack the ability to articulate them. It is especially common for children this age to act angry and aggressive or to express sadness by becoming withdrawn, rather than crying or talking about their feelings. These are normal reactions, but they should be addressed, particularly if they go on for several months. Anger and irritability can be signs of major depression in children, and extended periods of withdrawal can hamper a child's ability to form loving relationships later in life.

From Thirteen to Seventeen Years Old

Adolescents usually have an adult-like understanding of the reality and finality of death. They can think abstractly, and this ability makes them aware that death can happen to other people, and that it could also happen to them. They may experience and express a wide range of emotions, including denial, shock, anger, sadness, and withdrawal.

Teenagers and preteens are usually preoccupied with "fitting in" with their peer group. They may feel shame and embarrassment because the death of a parent makes them "stick out." One seventeen-year-old described sitting in class thinking of her mother's death and then worrying that her classmates could see inside her head to know exactly what she was thinking. Realizing her thoughts were unreasonable made her fear she was going crazy and that everyone around her knew it.

Though similar to adults in often being able to articulate complex emotions, adolescents are more likely than adults to act out their grief by behavior changes, such as over-eating, drinking, drug use, sexual promiscuity, or aggression. They may also react with anger and withdrawal. These are normal reactions, but don't ignore them. Appropriate discipline, tempered with understanding, keeps unhealthy behaviors from becoming entrenched patterns.

What You Can Do to Help

Get in Touch with Your Own Feelings

Many of the things you have learned about how to help your child cope with your illness can also help her cope with your death. Before you talk to your children about death, take some time to think about your own feelings about what is happening to you and about how your death will affect your family.

Saying out loud that you may be dying can be a harsh awakening; some people never actually believe it until they say it. Breaking this news to your children, who need you, may seem like an impossible task. You might want to practice what you are going to say, with your partner, therapist, or friend.

One mother wrote out an entire "script" of what to tell her children about her illness and her possible death. When the time came, she did not actually use the script, but she was prepared and knew what she wanted to say. "It would have been easier to just not do it," she said, "to just not tell them at all. I really had to force myself to accept that, as a parent, I cared most about what was important for their wellbeing, no matter how painful it was for me at the time."

Be Honest

It is critical that you talk honestly with your children about what you expect to happen. Early on, communicate the seriousness of your illness. If your prognosis changes, discuss it with them. Do not pretend that you will be getting better or that everything will be okay. Children know when things are not okay, and they will benefit from your honesty. In addition, if you know that you will not actually be okay, your child will be left with the burden of knowing you were not truthful with her about critical facts.

Avoid euphemisms, such as "Mommy is going to sleep" or "I am going on a long journey." Euphemisms may be particularly confusing to younger children who will take your words literally and expect you to "wake up" or "come home" after you are dead. On the other hand, they might expect to die if they go to sleep or be unable to return from a long trip.

Chances are, though, that your child is not truly aware that you are going to die. Children of all ages need their parents so much that they rarely allow themselves to accept death as a possibility even if intellectually they know that it is.

Tell your child all you know about the possible outcomes of your illness. Explain the medical aspects, the changes you may go through, and how long you are expected to live. At some point, you may want to bring your child to a doctor's appointment, preferably at the beginning or end of the day so that the doctor has more time, and let your doctor explain the medical issues so that you do not have to be the medical expert. This will take some of the pressure off you and will give your child a sense of security in hearing from a professional.

Communicate Openly
Make sure your children know that death is not a taboo subject in your home. Talk about how you are feeling and how you are coping. Be careful how you say things, though. No matter how understanding, mature, and intelligent your child may be, she will be emotionally injured if she is placed in the role of your confidant or counselor. No one can cope well all the time with the horrifying realization that they or someone they love will soon die. Be aware that it will be difficult to balance being open with your children while not being too dependent on them for emotional support.

Talk to your children about what you would like to accomplish during the time you have left and what you want and expect from them during this time. Make sure, though, that what you expect is realistic and relatively easy to accomplish. One bedridden mother asked her young children to paint pictures to brighten up her room. A dying father wanted more than anything to do things with his daughter that they both enjoyed, including going to an art exhibit. Some parents simply say they would like their children to go on doing the things they have always done, such as going to school and coming home to share stories about their day.

Death is scary, and nothing will take away your child's worries about losing you. Sometimes children make up illnesses so they won't have to go to school, fearing that their parent won't be there when they come home. Talk to your child about how she would like you to handle it if death becomes imminent while she is away. This will allow her to express her fears, and it will assure her that a plan is in place in case of an emergency.

Most children are frightened by the uncertainty of what their future will hold if their parents are not around to take care of them. If you talk honestly with your children, allowing and encouraging them to express their thoughts, feelings, and fears, they will feel more secure. Let them know that they will be safe and taken care of. If you need to make specific changes to ensure that they are cared for, let them know what these changes are and that their input about these changes will be heard. For example, one father had to figure out how his children would be cared for during his frequent business trips after his wife died. He let the children know they would stay at their grandparents' house whenever he was out of town. After they tried this plan a few times, though, the children realized they needed the secure feeling they got in their own home. The father responded to their feelings and arranged for the grandparents to stay with them in their own house when he travelled.

For Young Children: Explain What Death Means

If your child is very young, probably the most pressing question she will have is why someone has to die at all. Explain that every living thing eventually dies. You can illustrate this point by telling her that coats, umbrellas, and toys don't die, but plants, animals, and people do. Let her know that there is something called a life span, which is the amount of time a person or thing is expected to live. Most people live for a long time. Nowadays women usually live to be about eighty-seven years old, and men usually live to be about eighty-four. Some people die much younger than that, either because they get sick or because they get badly hurt.

If your child asks if she will die, answer her truthfully but also let her know that she has a whole life ahead of her. While some people live to be one-hundred years old, others don't live to be fifty. But all things must die because they live.

For young children who have trouble understanding that death is permanent, you might want to explain that, when death takes place, the body stops working, and it will never work again. Since the body is no longer living, it cannot talk or walk ever again but it also does not feel pain anymore. When someone dies, the brain stops working and never starts working again. Be prepared to explain this many times, because there is no clear and easy way for a child to grasp such a difficult concept.

Your child may also have spiritual or religious questions about death. Share your own religious views about what death means with your child, and let her share her views with you. You may also want to explain that different cultures believe different things about heaven and the spirit and whether there is an afterlife.

Help Your Child Find Support

If your child does not want to talk about the illness or the possibility of your death, be respectful of her needs, but remind her from time to time that you are open to discussion and that any feelings she has are acceptable to you, even negative ones.

Your child may refrain from telling you her feelings out of a desire to protect you. Ask your child what might help her cope with her feelings. She may feel safer talking to someone with some distance from the problem, such as a counselor. You might want to ask her if she would be interested in counseling and, if so, make the necessary arrangements. Many children, especially teenagers, may benefit from grief support groups with peers who have experienced loss. Let your child know it is okay to talk to friends and other family members if she feels uncomfortable discussing her feelings with you.

Offer her some ideas for coping such as journaling or writing a letter to you. Sometimes writing feelings down is easier and feels safer than saying them out loud. Many children benefit from reading books with you, drawing pictures to help them express their feelings, or doing art projects. Children of all ages will benefit from extra attention, nurturing, and physical contact, all of which make them feel safe and loved.

Be Alert to Changing Roles in the Family

As a result of a parent's death, children's roles in the family may change. If this will happen in your family, talk to your child about what her new role or responsibilities might be, and give her as much time as possible to get used to them. Remember that children have certain things they need to do to become healthy and happy adults, including going to school, playing, forming relationships with friends, and relying on their parent or guardian for emotional support and guidance.

Again, do not tell your children that they will have to be the "man of the house" or the "mother" to younger siblings. Their emotional health will be jeopardized if they are forced to grow up too soon or to play the role of surrogate parent or spouse. Children can be asked to help more with the housework or the babysitting, though, without compromising their childhood. It is a delicate balance that requires thought and planning. Many parents find it helpful to talk over what new roles their children might be expected to play in the family with therapists, clergy, or other trusted adults.

Create Messages for Special Occasions

It is terrible to think that you might not live to see special events and occasions in your child's future. Your planning can help your child through important events for the rest of her life. If you know that you may be dying, you can prepare messages for special occasions in your child's life. You can write letters or make videos for your child to review on important dates, such as graduations, weddings, and childbirth. You may want to write your memoirs for the family to read at special times.

You may want to go through your belongings and specify whom you wish to get certain things. It can be a great comfort for a child to have some of her parent's personal belongings, particularly if she knows that her parent wanted her to have something specific. Alice, a young woman whose mother died several years ago, said, "I wear my mother's wedding band every day. It makes me feel connected to her, and I love knowing that she wanted me to have it."

Don't expect your spouse or others to know what you want to happen. Planning ahead will ensure your wishes are clear and prevent confusion and disagreement within your family. It also gives your family a positive way to stay connected to you.

Consider Planning Your Funeral

If you can garner enough physical and emotional strength, try to plan at least some aspects of your own funeral. There is nothing you can do to take away your child's grief and pain. Careful preparation, though, can help your entire family cope with their loss and can also bring you peace of mind. Doing so increases the chances that your family will follow your wishes, and it will clarify what role, if any, you expect your children to play in your funeral. One mother decided what she would wear for her funeral, selected the music, and specified who would speak. In a letter to her husband, she wrote: "I couldn't stand the thought of you and the children having to make these decisions, trying to guess what I would want. Please keep it simple and just be there for each other."

Dos and Don'ts for Coping with Your Terminal Illness

- *Don't* expect your young child to know your illness is terminal or to understand that death is permanent. Even older children may not fully grasp the meaning of death.

- *Don't* be surprised if your children act unaffected at first when you share the news that your illness is terminal. This defense is normal in children who must first come to grips with the intensity of their emotions.

- *Do* reassure your child she will be taken care of and it is normal for her to feel scared or worried.

- *Do* encourage your child to talk about her feelings. Let her know how you feel, too.

- *Do* recognize that your children will worry about their basic needs being met. It is normal for them to worry about how their lives will be affected by your death.

- *Don't* get angry if your child seems selfish or expresses concerns that seem trivial.

- *Don't* ask your child to fill a role in the family that she is not old enough, emotionally or developmentally, to handle.

- *Do* try to maintain as much routine as possible in your children's lives.

- *Don't* think that because you have answered a question once, your child won't ask the same question repeatedly, especially younger children.

- *Do* think ahead about how to talk to your children about your prognosis and your feelings about it.

- *Do* plan ahead for special occasions in your children's lives that you will not share.

- *Do* consider writing letters, making videos, and designating special mementos for your family to have when you are gone.

Hospice

If you have learned that your illness is likely to be terminal, one option you and your family may want to consider is hospice care. Hospice is a specific type of care that offers services for families with a dying member. According to the National Hospice Foundation, the goal of hospice is to offer a team-oriented approach to the medical care, pain management, and emotional and spiritual support of the dying patient and his family. It is intended to allow the patient a pain-free way to die with dignity.

The focus of hospice is on care, not cure, and most of the care takes place in the home. Services are offered without any restrictions based on age, religion, race, or illness. You may find a local hospice through your hospitals and nursing homes or by looking in the telephone book or online for a local freestanding hospice facility. According to David Techner, Director of the Kaufman Chapel in Detroit, Michigan,

> *Most people are much more comfortable at home with friends and family around than they are in the hospital. Hospice recognizes that the disease has won, that there is nothing more that you can do to treat the disease, and now it is time to focus on controlling the pain. The person who is dying then gets to be comfortable for the rest of their time here.*

Many hospices offer therapeutic services to all family members. You may want to speak with hospice counselors to get help in explaining to your children that hospice is geared not toward finding a cure for your illness but toward making your final days as comfortable as possible.

9. Going On: Notes for the Surviving Parent

This book is about *surviving* a serious illness. The sad reality, though, is that sometimes illness is terminal. Those left behind may feel overwhelmed by their grief, and the surviving parent faces a new role as a single parent. We usually don't expect our loved ones to die, and we can never fully prepare to lose them, especially prematurely. At the height of their grief, newly single parents are often asked to take on unfamiliar tasks that were previously their partner's responsibility. One man whose wife died unexpectedly after a brief illness told us, "I know this is a strange thing to think about at a time like this, but I keep thinking about how terrified I am to go grocery shopping. I have no idea how to shop for four kids because my wife always did that."

Talking to Your Child about Funerals

When a loved one dies, you are faced with some immediate and tangible demands, such as the logistics of the funeral. For many people these demands are welcome tasks, providing something concrete to grasp onto when everything seems nebulous and one's whole life seems to have been dismantled. Try to find ways to include your children in this process since they too are bound to feel at a loss about what to do next. You can start by explaining the decisions about the funeral and burial.

You may need to explain to a very young child exactly what a funeral is. You might want to tell him that when a person's body stops working, someone has to decide what to do with the body. This decision usually falls on the family, and most families choose burial or cremation.

Burial

Young children may wonder why we bury a person's body and what will happen to it in the ground or in a mausoleum vault. Explain that once the body is put there, it stays there, and that never changes. Though we can't see the body anymore, the grave or mausoleum becomes the place that people can visit to pray for or simply remember their loved one. Some children will need a technical explanation of what happens to the body after it is buried. If your child specifically asks for details, you can tell him that the body decays, leaving only bones. If you believe the spirit lives on, or that there is an afterlife, this might be a good time to explain your beliefs about that as well.

Cremation

If the body is to be cremated, explain what cremation is and why it has been chosen. Give the simplest and most direct explanation you can about the choice. Point out that cremation, like underground or above-ground burial, is common all over the world and that it is chosen for personal, cultural, religious, and even environmental reasons. The thought of a parent's body being burned can be scary for children, so you will want to remind them that once the body stops working, nothing will ever hurt it again. For some children, cremation will be less frightening than burial, knowing that the body will not be subject to decay.

Attending the Funeral or Memorial Service

Our experience as therapists has convinced us that children of all ages, including the very young, should attend a parent's funeral or memorial service. Some experts, however, feel that babies and toddlers should not attend funerals. We believe that attending the funeral or memorial service allows children to begin to accept the reality of death and to say goodbye in a formal way. Even very young children who do not understand or remember much about the ceremony will be grateful to have been there when they are older. Children sometimes get frightened or overwhelmed at a parent's funeral, though, especially in the presence of the corpse, so you might want to ask a friend or family member to attend to your child if necessary. Consider having a video of the funeral made and asking for a copy of the eulogy. While many families do not think to keep records of this kind, they can offer consolation to children later whether they attended the funeral or not.

If a child objects to attending, respect his wishes. In that event, you might plan some sort of alternative memorial ceremony as soon as the child is ready, even if just the two of you attend. If you have ever experienced the death of a pet, you may know the consolation children find in making up rituals for them. Children who are too distressed to attend a parent's funeral are often sad or angry with themselves later in their lives; a special ceremony can help ease those regrets.

If your child does not object to attending the funeral, describe what to expect. Let him know where the casket will be, whether there will be an open casket and, if so, how the body will be dressed. Will there be a hearse for the casket? Who else will be there? Who will take him to the ceremony? Will the family ride in a limousine to the cemetery? Who will the pallbearers be? What type of music will be played? Explain where he will sit and what will be expected of him. Will he be expected to view the body or kiss it? You might warn him that the corpse may not look or feel like the person did in life. If he seems frightened by any of this, assure him that he won't have to do anything that makes him feel uncomfortable.

In a cremation ceremony, an urn will be on display instead of a casket during the ceremony. You should explain that this will contain his parent's ashes. You will also want to say what will be done with the urn and the ashes after the funeral, whether they will be distributed or saved in some special place.

Keeping It Together

Undoubtedly, you and your family will not be "normal" for a while because you will be grieving for your loved one. You may never really feel "normal" again. One young woman, recalling her mother's death, said, "It never felt normal to sit at the dinner table again. We were only three, and we used to be four." It is important to accept the fact that healing from a great loss takes time; denying this reality will only cause delayed grief that will reemerge eventually. The problem with being a grieving parent is that in spite of your own pain you have to be strong enough to take care of your children and help them deal with their sorrow. If they think you can't handle your feelings, they won't trust you with the intensity of theirs.

For some people, it helps to make a list of your priorities for the children after the funeral. You might need to write down that you want them to return to school by a certain date. You might want to ask them which possessions of their deceased parent they would like to keep as a remembrance, if that has not already been determined. It helps to remind yourself frequently that you will on occasion fall down on the job, and that's okay. Consider writing down the names of those people you feel are willing and able to help you with your parenting duties, whether it is by providing emotional support, emergency babysitting, housekeeping, or grocery shopping when you feel you can't handle things. Even if it is hard for you to accept help from others, call these people when you need help; keep in mind that it will benefit them as well by giving them a way to express their love for your family during their own time of grieving.

For some families, the end of a lengthy illness can bring a sense of relief. You may be grateful that your partner's suffering has ended, particularly if the illness has been prolonged and painful. If you react this way, do not be ashamed or embarrassed, and normalize your children's reactions if they also experience these emotions. You may want to tell your child that these feelings are an indication of their love for their parent, not their insensitivity.

Handling Intense Sadness
After the funeral, you and your children will no doubt be faced with intense feelings of sadness. Sorrow sometimes makes people feel out of control, especially if they are unable to stop crying or if they become physically ill because of their grief. Crying itself is not a weakness but a normal reaction to the death of a loved one. When you cry in front of your child, you are modeling a healthy way to express strong emotions. Still, it will be hard to watch your children grieve, knowing there is no way you can "fix" their pain.

You can do much to help them deal with their feelings, though, by letting them know that their grieving is natural and that they won't always hurt like they are hurting right now. You may want to discuss with your child the options about what he can do if he feels overwhelmed with grief in a place that does not feel safe to him. For example, if he starts getting distressed in class and doesn't want to break down in front of his peers, he can visit the school counselor. Also, you can give your child extra physical affection and love in the months immediately following the funeral. Remind yourself and your child that the intensity of these feelings will lessen with time, although you may still find unexpected things plunging you back into sorrow. Be prepared to break down occasionally. While we never completely get over the death of a loved one, we eventually learn to live with it.

Dealing with Misplaced Anger

You may feel at times that you cannot compete with your deceased spouse, who may be idealized in your child's mind. Your child might be angry or resentful that you are still here, while his other parent is not. It is not easy being the target of a child's anger, however misplaced, but try not to take it personally or react defensively. Recognize that your child is searching for ways to express his pain and that directing his anger at you is actually a vote of confidence in you as a safe place to direct it.

Most children express anger in one way or another as part of the grieving process. Toddlers might become more aggressive with you or other children and might begin hitting and biting. School-aged children may become more aggressive, physically or verbally. Some begin cursing, using words you didn't know they knew. Teen boys may hit walls or get in fights; teen girls tend to turn their anger inward. Grieving adolescent girls may be at risk for self-destructive behavior such as eating disorders, sexual promiscuity, or substance abuse.

Make sure you take action quickly if you see your child doing something that might hurt him or others. Understand that his behavior is the result of loss, but don't let that stop you from disciplining him. Take whatever action you would have taken if your partner had not died, but temper it with plenty of affection. You might tell your toddler something simple like, "I get frustrated a lot, too, because I'm so sad that Daddy died. But it's not okay to bite when we get frustrated, so you need to go to Time Out for a few minutes to cool off. Next time you get mad, try coming to me or your teacher for a hug instead."

Ask an older child what he thinks motivated his destructive behavior, and how he might cope with his feelings in other ways. Make suggestions of your own. For example, when he's feeling bad he might come talk to you, take a bike ride, or call a friend. If he has frequent angry outbursts, consider counseling. After all, anyone who has gone through a crisis like the one he is going through would welcome having someone who can understand him and help him.

Whatever your child's age, let him know that you understand he is angry, and that his feelings are normal. Tell him that you feel angry, too. Let him know that the two of you will get through this together. If you overreact to your child's outbursts with intense anger of your own, you might want to leave the room for a few minutes, take some deep breaths, think through what you want to say, and return when you are calmer. If you frequently find yourself overwhelmed by the intensity of your child's emotions, consider talking to a counselor or a clergy member yourself. What is good advice for your child is often good advice for you.

All in Due Time...
There are many things you can do with your family to help cope with your shared loss. If possible, consider taking some time off work to concentrate on working through your grief and developing what is sure to be a new relationship with your

children. Otherwise, try as much as possible to maintain the normal routines in the house. Talk to your children about what they can do to help at home. But remember to be realistic about how much will get done. Let up on the housekeeping a bit. Talk to other adults in your child's life about temporarily easing up on their expectations in the classroom, on the playing field, or even in friendships. If you can afford it, hire a housekeeper. If that is not feasible, ask friends and family to help out.

If possible, try to put off big changes for at least a year. It is easy to make rash, emotional decisions at the beginning of the grieving process that you might regret later. Even if you feel ready to make changes, your child will need time to adjust.

People often decide to move to a new house following the death of a loved one. This decision is often motivated by emotional factors like the desire to start over in a place not so loaded with memories, or practical ones like finances. If you are considering a move, be sure to discuss with your children the emotional impact of such a move and include them in the decision-making process. Give them the opportunity to express their opinions. If you do move, give them some choices, like which room will be theirs or what color it will be painted.

Eventually you may want to begin dating, but you should not rush into a new long-term relationship. You may feel overwhelmed and lonely, and the idea of a new partner may be appealing. In addition to meeting your own emotional needs, a partner might offer your children all the advantages of a second parent. Remember, however, that you and your children need adequate time to grieve and heal from your loss before you introduce someone new as a permanent fixture in your lives.

Another point to consider is when and how to pack up your partner's belongings. Everyone has a different timeline as to when they are ready to dispose of a loved one's clothes and other personal items. Some people want to do it right away as a means of beginning the healing process. Others choose to wait months and even years before they pack things up. We have all seen the movie or heard the story about the room that becomes a taboo museum of memories of the deceased, and we instinctively know that in such a scenario there is something amiss. There will be people who pressure you to get rid of things quickly, and others who would have you save everything forever, but remember there is no perfect time to handle these affairs. There is only the time that is right for you and your family.

The important thing to remember is that when you are ready to gather your partner's things, let your children know ahead of time. Ask them how they feel about it. Let them select items for themselves, and offer them a say in where the remaining items should go. Be sensitive to the fact that this will be a painful experience for everyone. If your children do not want to keep any personal items, respect their decision, but also consider holding aside a few items you think they might want at a future time, in case they have second thoughts later. One woman who lost her mother as a teen said,

> *It was really hard to make those decisions about what to keep and what to give away, and I felt like I had to make the decision quickly. I kept obvious things like jewelry, but I wish I had kept more clothes and shoes and bags, things I might have wanted when I got older or just liked having to keep me feeling close to my mother as I aged.*

To work through the grieving process, some families establish rituals such as visiting the gravesite on special days, attending religious services, saying a prayer, or listening to a song. Some families establish a memorial to the deceased parent. Talk to your children about what might make them feel connected to the deceased, and devise a family plan. Doing so will give your children something to hold onto later in life when they are missing their parent. One daughter told us that she takes yellow roses, her mother's favorite flower, to the cemetery on her mother's birthday and on the anniversary of her death. Another woman whose father died when she was a teen told us she goes to her father's favorite restaurant and orders his favorite meal of a reuben sandwich and a Guinness on his birthday every year.

Chances are your children's grief will be reawakened at each stage of their lives and at milestones such as the birthday and the anniversary of the deceased parent's death. Sadness may also arise at their own birthdays, graduations, and weddings, and at the births of their own children. Buying a first home, getting a first job, and other significant life events may trigger feelings of loss as well, anything that a child might have wanted to share with her parent. One woman recalls cleaning out her father's attic years after her mother's death. Coming across a box with her mother's belongings, she burst into tears when she breathed the fragrance of an old sweater her mother wore.

Special occasions may also trigger intense memories and strong emotions. While some people might avoid talking about the loved one they miss at these times, opening up about the absence of a loved one can be a way of including them in the event even though they are no longer alive. As one father said,

I told my daughter I wished her mother was here to help her pick out her wedding dress, and she burst into tears. At

first, I thought I'd made a mistake, but we were able to talk about how sad she was that her mother wasn't here to share in this wonderful occasion. Talking about it openly helped both of us.

Talking about feelings of loss at key moments is a positive way of addressing the emotions. Pretending that they don't exist only doubles the sense of loss. Ignoring sadness gives other family members the impression that one doesn't care or that their own feelings don't matter, when actually including those feelings in joyous occasions can intensify the joy. As one mother explained,

Every joyous occasion is now an alloy of joy and pain. I loved seeing my son graduate from college, but it was bittersweet because his father was not there. I loved seeing the birth of my first grandchild, but again, he was not there. Talking about it keeps the pain under control and helps us preserve his memory. So, in fact, it is like he is with us for each important event.

During peak emotional times when you and your children miss your spouse, try telling stories about his or her life. Remember her, look at pictures, and talk about how much you miss her. Wonder aloud at what she might say or do during a special event. Ask your children to share their memories, and let them know how much their deceased parent would have wanted to share in their lives. Let them know how proud you are of them and how proud their other parent would be, too.

Dos and Don'ts for **Going On**

- *Do* talk about the funeral arrangements with your child.

- *Do* explain to your young child what a funeral is and what he can expect to happen.

- *Do* encourage your child to attend the funeral, even if only briefly. Tell him friends or family members will be there to support him, and it is okay if he wants to leave.

- *Don't* force your child to attend the funeral if he doesn't want to.

- *Do* take people up on their offers to help, and specify what they can do for your family. Make a list of things you need done and get someone to help delegate responsibilities.

- *Do* recognize that your children are searching for ways to express their pain. Be sensitive to their feelings, but also continue to set limits and discipline them.

- *Do* let your child know what you are feeling, and ask him about his feelings. Let him know that whatever he is feeling is okay and you are there for him if he wants to talk.

- *Don't* tell your child to stop crying; crying is a normal expression of grief.

- *Do* maintain as much routine in your household as possible. Children need stability and the comfort of routines to feel safe and secure.

- *Don't* make major changes in your life such as moving or remarrying for at least a year (if possible).

- *Do* establish family rituals to remember the deceased parent.

- *Don't* think that not talking about the deceased parent will protect your child from pain. Children need to hear stories about their dead parent, and they need to know that it is okay to share their memories.

- *Don't* expect your or your children's grief to follow a timeline. Everyone heals differently.

10. Conclusion

Thank you for reading our book. We hope you have found suggestions that will guide you and your family through a challenging period. We know there is no way for us to answer all of your questions or solve all of your problems. We hope, though, that this book has pointed out ways for you to help yourself and your family. We are grateful to all of the families who shared their stories with us, and we hope that in hearing their experiences you have found some comfort.

As we have mentioned, many challenges—both physical and emotional—arise when a family member is seriously ill. The challenges don't disappear, even with a full recovery. Children can be left with the fear that one of their parents might get sick again. Partners can feel the same fear and may try to protect themselves emotionally from future loss. Negative emotions linked to your illness may well linger. As one man told us,

> *I only realized recently that after my surgery I withdrew emotionally from my family because I was depressed. It's two years later, and I suddenly realize that I have a lot of catching up to do. I've had to have some frank discussions with my children and with my wife. I'm in individual therapy, and we're in marriage counseling. The thing is, though, that we've identified the problem, and we're going to work through it. We've already worked through so much together.*

We are confident that you, too, can work through the challenges your family faces. It might help to recall the problems that you and your family have already worked through together. Hopefully, the lines of communication that have been opened as a result of your illness will remain open so that you can discuss any lingering fears family members may have. Even years after your recovery, you may still need to talk about what you and your family have gone through. One woman who was eighteen when her mother recovered from breast cancer told us that talking with her parents ten years later about their experiences with the illness opened new avenues of communication and gave them insight into some unresolved feelings.

Throughout your illness, you and your family have no doubt changed and probably grown stronger in many ways. You have learned things about—and from—each other. You have probably learned things from others who have been through some experiences similar to your own. Everyone's experience is unique, so you may have had to tailor any advice you've received to your own situation. Having gone through your crisis, you are probably in a good position to help others now. We have certainly learned much from those who have shared their stories for this book, as well as from those who read the first edition of this book and gave their feedback on what was useful and what might be improved.

Above all, we—Leigh and Courtney—hope this book has provided some peace and comfort for your family during a difficult time.

Appendix A

Suggested Writing Exercises

Most people who are seriously ill feel hopeless at times. Research indicates, though, that the recovery process is hastened when people have hope and understand that their lives have meaning. Writing exercises can be a good way to remind you of what is important and meaningful in your life. They can also be a good way to communicate your thoughts, feelings, and values to your family. Consider sharing your writings with your family members. They can provide good springboards to important conversations.

Exercise One

1. What are your earliest memories?

2. When you were a child, who was an adult who influenced you and how?

3. What is a mistake you made during your adolescence that taught you an important lesson?

4. What is something that makes you very proud?

5. What is the best thing that ever happened to you?

6. List and discuss the top three things that give your life meaning?

7. Would this list have been different if you were writing it before you became ill? If so, how?

8. What would you like your child's life to look like in five years? Ten? Twenty?

9. What would you like your life to be like in five years? Ten? Twenty?

10. What changes, if any, has your illness had on what you value and want out of life?

Exercise Two

Write a letter to your children. Some things you might want to include in the letter are:

- Things about them that you love

- What you want out of life for them

- Important details about your life, such as how you felt on your wedding day and when they were born, as well as things that interest you, such as travel, art, sports, movies, baking, etc.

- Things you enjoy doing with them now or enjoyed doing with them in the past

- Things you would like to do with them now or in the future

- How your life has changed since you became ill

When you write a letter, it doesn't have to be a work of art; most aren't. The most important function of a letter is to help you communicate with someone. It doesn't have to flow in a particular way, and your grammar doesn't have to be perfect.

You might start simply by saying something like: "I'm sitting here, thinking about you, and I decided to write you a letter."

Some people keep a journal in which they regularly write letters to their children with this type of information. Whether you let your children read it now or later in their lives, it can provide them with a window into your life that they may not have had access to otherwise. Older children report that they treasure this kind of gift from their parents.

Going It Alone: Suggested Writing Exercises for Single Parents

1. Write a letter to someone you feel close to (such as a relative or close friend) outlining all of your financial information. This should include your will, life insurance, home or medical insurance policies, and other financial holdings. This letter should include account numbers, bank statements, and medical history, as well as names and numbers of people to talk to for assistance. It will ease your mind as you go through treatments to know that this information is organized and that someone will handle your affairs if the need arises. Tell the person to whom you wrote the letter where they can find it if they need it.

2. What is your single greatest accomplishment as a single parent?

3. Consider keeping a journal in which you include daily notes about your feelings and experiences, letters to your children, your wishes and fears, or anything else that feels useful.

Appendix B

Resources

American Association of Pastoral Counselors
9504A Lee Highway
Fairfax, VA 22031-2303
(703)385-6967
www.aapc.org

American Bar Association
740 15th Street NW
Washington, D.C. 20005
(202)662-1000
www.americanbar.org

American Cancer Society
1599 Clifton Road
Atlanta, GA 30329
(800)ACS-2345
www.cancer.org

American Diabetes Association
1701 N. Beauregard Street
Alexandria, VA 22311
(800)342-2383
www.diabetes.org

American Heart Association
National Center
7272 Greenville Avenue
Dallas, TX 75231
(800)AHA-USA1
www.americanheart.org

American Stroke Association
5916 Dearborn Street
Mission, KS 66202
(913)649-1776

Association of Jewish Family and Children's Agencies
5750 Park Heights Avenue
Baltimore, MD 21215
(800)634-7346
www.ajfca.org

Care Calendar
http://www.carecalendar.org/

Caring Bridges
http://www.caringbridge.org/

Centers for Medicare and Medicaid Services
7500 Security Boulevard
Baltimore, MD 21244-1850
(410)786-3000
www.medicaid.gov
www.medicaid.aphsa.org

Child Welfare League of America
1726 M St. NW, Suite 500
Washington, D.C. 20036
(202)688-4200
www.cwla.org

U.S. Department of Health and Human Services
200 Independence Avenue, S.W.; Room 443 H
Washington, D.C. 20201
www.aids.gov

FORCE: Facing Our Risk of Cancer Empowered
16057 Tampa Palms Blvd. W, PMB #373
Tampa, FL 33647
(866)288-7475
www.facingourrisk.org

Good Grief Program
BU School of Medicine
Vose Hall, 4th Floor
88 East Concord Street
Boston, MA 02118
(617)414-4005

Hospice Foundation of America
1710 Rhode Island Avenue, NW, Suite 400
Washington, D.C. 20036
(202)457-5811; (800)854-3402
www.hospicefoundation.org

Kids Konnected
26071 Merit Circle, Suite 103
Laguna Hills, CA 92653
(949)582-5443; (800)899-2866
www.kidskonnected.org

Susan G. Komen for the Cure
5005 LBJ Freeway, Suite 250
Dallas, TX 75244
(877)465-6636
www.komen.org

Lupus Foundation of America, Inc.
2000 L Street, N.W., Suite 410
Washington, DC 20036
(202)349-1155
www.lupus.org

Multiple Sclerosis Association of America
375 Kings Highway North
Cherry Hill, NJ 08034
(800)532-7667; (856)488-4500
email: *msaa@mymsaa.org*
www.msaa.com

National Hospice Foundation
www.hospiceinfo.org

National Multiple Sclerosis Society
733 Third Avenue
New York, NY 10017
(800)Fight MS
(800)344-4867
www.nmss.org

National Society of Genetic Counselors, Inc.
330 N. Wabash Avenue, Suite 2000
Chicago, IL 60611
(312)321-6834
www.nsgc.org

Social Security Disability Legal Help
www.social-security-benefits.com

Transplant Recipients International Organization, Inc.
13705 Currant Loop
Gainesville, VA 20155-3031
(800)874-6386
Email: *info@trioweb.org*
www.trioweb.org

United Way of America
701 North Fairfax Street
Alexandria, VA 22314
(703)836-7112
www.unitedway.org

U.S. Department of Health and Human Services
200 Independence Avenue, S.W.
Washington, D.C. 20201
(877)696-6775
www.hhs.gov/healthcare

Appendix C

Recommended Reading

For Children and Teens

Ackerman, A. (2001). *Our mom has cancer*. Atlanta, GA: American Cancer Society.

American Cancer Society (2002). *Because...Someone I love has cancer: Kids' activity book*. Atlanta, GA: American Cancer Society.

Bunting, E. (1982). *The happy funeral*. New York, NY: Harper Collins.

Carney, K.L. (1998). *What is cancer anyway? Explaining cancer to children of all ages*. Edmond, OK: Dragonfly Publishing.

Clark, J.A. (2010). *You are the best medicine*. New York, NY: Balzer & Bray.

Frahm, A. & Schultz, E. (2001). *Tickles Tabitha's cancer-tankerous mommy*. Raleigh, NC: Nutcracker Publishing.

Glader, S. (2013). *Nowhere hair: Explains your cancer and chemo to your kids*. Mill Valley, CA: Thousand Words Press.

Grollman, E.A. (2014*). Straight talk about death for teenagers: How to cope with losing someone you love*. Boston, MA: Beacon Press.

Heegard, M. (1992). *When someone has a very serious illness: Children can learn to cope with loss and change*. Minneapolis, MN: Woodland Press.

Kohlenberg, S. & Crow, L. (1993). *Sammy's mommy has cancer*. Washington, DC: Magination Press/American Psychological Association.

Lewis, A. (2005). *When someone you love has cancer: A guide to help kids cope.* St. Meinrad, IN: Abbey Press.

Martin, C. & Martin, C. (2016). *The rainbow feelings of cancer: A book for children who have a loved one with cancer.* Chino Valley, AZ: Hohm Press.

McVicker, E. (2015). *Butterfly kisses and wishes on wings: when someone you love has cancer…a hopeful, helpful book for kids.* Aurora, CO: McVicker & Hersh.

Moore-Mallinos, J. (2008). *Mom has cancer!* Hauppauge, NY: Barron Educational Series.

Numeroff, L. & Harpham, W.S. (1999). *Kids talk: Kids speak out about breast cancer.* New York, NY: Samsung Telecommunications America.

O'Toole, D.B. (1995). *Facing change: Falling apart and coming together again in the teen years.* Burnsville, NC: Compassion Books.

Parkinson, C.S. (1991). *My mommy has cancer.* New York, NY: Park Press.

Silver, M. & Silver, M. (2013). *My parent has cancer and it really sucks.* Chicago, IL: Sourcebooks Fire.

Tiffault, B. (1992). *A quilt for Elizabeth.* Omaha, NE: Centering Corporation.

For Parents

Bernhard, T. (2015). *How to live well with chronic pain and illness: A mindful guide.* Somerville, MA: Wisdom Publications.

Decker, J. (2014). *Fight like a mother: How to be a mom with a chronic illness.* Printed by CreateSpace.

Grollman, E. (1990). *Talking about death: A dialogue between parent and child.* Boston, MA: Beacon Press.

Harris, M. (1995). *The loss that is forever: The lifelong impact of the early death of a mother or father.* New York, NY: Penguin Books.

Heiney, S.P. (2001). *Cancer in the family: Helping children cope with a parent's death.* American Cancer Society.

Horn, D. (2013). *Chronic resilience:10 sanity-saving tools for women coping with the stress of illness.* Newburyport, MA: Conari Press.

Kübler-Ross, E. (1997). *To live until we say goodbye.* New York, NY: Scribner.

Kübler-Ross, E. & Bycock, I. (2014). *On death and dying: What the dying have to teach doctors, nurses, clergy and their own families.* New York, NY: Scribner.

Kushner, H.S. (1997). *When bad things happen to good people.* New York, NY: Avon Publishing.

Martin, C. (2000). *Writing your way through cancer.* Chino Valley, AZ: Hohm Press.

McCue, K. & Bonn, R. (2011). *How to help children through a parent's serious illness: Supportive, practical advice from a leading child life specialist.* New York, NY: St. Martin's Griffin.

Monahan, C. (1993). *Children and trauma: A guide for parents and professionals.* San Francisco, CA: Josey-Bass.

Nussbaum, K. (1998). *Preparing the children: Information and ideas for families facing terminal illness and death.* Kodiak: Gifts of Hope Trust.

National Institutes of Health (1995). *When someone in your family has cancer.* Bethesda, MD: National Cancer Institute.

Overman, S.S. (2012). *You don't look sick!: Living well with chronic invisible illness.* New York, NY: Demos Health.

Rauch, P. & Muriel, A. (2005). *Raising an emotionally healthy child when a parent is sick.* New York, NY: McGraw-Hill.

Trozzi, M. & Massimini, K. (1999*). Talking with children about loss: Words, strategies, and wisdom to help children cope with death, divorce, and other difficult times.* New York, NY: Penguin Putnam.

Ulbrich, C. (2011). *How can you NOT laugh at a time like this?: Reclaim your health with humor, creativity, and grit.* New Haven, CT: Tell Me Press.

Index

About the Authors

LEIGH COLLINS, LCSW, teaches in the Social Work Department at California State University, Bakersfield. She received her MSW from Tulane University in 1998 and is licensed as a clinical social worker in California and Louisiana. Before beginning her teaching career, Leigh worked for many years as a child and adolescent therapist and a school social worker. She is married and has one child.

COURTNEY NATHAN, LCSW, is a licensed clinical social worker in New Orleans. She is the founder of the Professional Development Network, a company providing high quality, affordable continuing education for mental health professionals in the New Orleans area. Courtney earned her MSW from Tulane University in 1993. Before opening her own business, she worked as a therapist for several years, specializing in treatment of adolescents and young adult women. Courtney is married with two children.

Contact Information: Please "like" us on Facebook. You can send us private messages through our page, "Parenting through Illness."

About Hohm Press

HOHM PRESS (and our affiliate **Kalindi Press**) is committed to publishing books that provide readers with alternatives to the materialistic values of the current culture, and promote self-awareness, the recognition of interdependence, and compassion. Our subject areas include parenting, transpersonal psychology, religious studies, women's studies, the arts and poetry. **KALINDI PRESS** is proud to present the Family and World Health series, for parents and children, as well as books for adults that focus on health and wellbeing.

Contact Information: Hohm Press, PO Box 4410, Chino Valley, Arizona, 86323; USA; 800-381-2700, or 928-636-3331; email: *publisher@hohmpress.com*

Visit our websites at *www.hohmpress.com /*
www.familyhealthseries.com / www.kalindipress.com